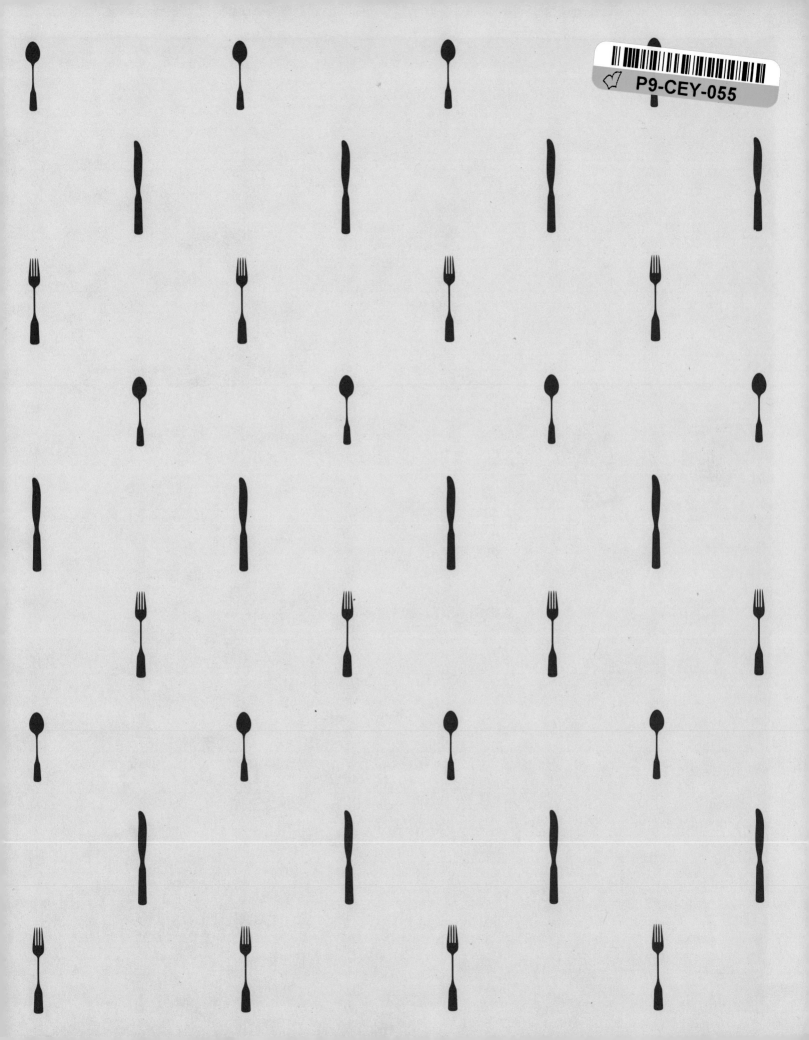

Fresh Ways with Cakes

Time-Life Books Inc.
is a wholly owned subsidiary of

TIME INCORPORATED

FOUNDER: Henry R. Luce 1898-1967

Editor-in-Chief: Jason McManus
Chairman and Chief Executive Officer: J. Richard Munro
President and Chief Operating Officer: N. J. Nicholas, Jr.
Editorial Director: Ray Cave
Executive Vice President, Books: Kelso F. Sutton
Vice President, Books: George Artandi

COVER
Embellished with a lattice of caramelized sugar (technique, page 18) and two layers of filling, Mango Slices (recipe, page 124) are deceptively rich-looking. While traditional cake fillings depend on high-calorie ingredients for flavor, lively taste and color are achieved here in a layer of fresh raspberry puree (recipe, page 15) thickened with unflavored gelatin. Fresh mangoes, skim milk, and egg white combine in a second layer to create an airy custard that adds few calories. For a total of only 107 calories per serving, Mango Slices provide an elegant and satisfying dessert.

TIME-LIFE BOOKS INC.
EDITOR: George Constable
Executive Editor: Ellen Phillips
Director of Design: Louis Klein
Director of Editorial Resources: Phyllis K. Wise
Editorial Board: Russell B. Adams, Jr., Dale M. Brown, Roberta Conlan, Thomas H. Flaherty, Lee Hassig, Donia Ann Steele, Rosalind Stubenberg, Kit van Tulleken, Henry Woodhead
Director of Photography and Research: John Conrad Weiser

EUROPEAN EDITOR: Kit van Tulleken
Assistant European Editor: Gillian Moore
Design Director: Ed Skyner
Chief of Research: Vanessa Kramer
Chief Sub-Editor: Ilse Gray

PRESIDENT: Christopher T. Linen
Chief Operating Officer: John M. Fahey, Jr.
Senior Vice President: James L. Mercer
Vice Presidents: Stephen L. Bair, Ralph J. Cuomo, Neal Goff, Stephen L. Goldstein, Juanita T. James, Hallett Johnson III, Carol Kaplan, Susan J. Maruyama, Robert H. Smith, Paul R. Stewart, Joseph J. Ward
Director of Production Services: Robert J. Passantino

HEALTHY HOME COOKING

SERIES DIRECTOR: Jackie Matthews
Picture Editor: Mark Karras
Editorial Assistant: Eugénie Romer

Editorial Staff for *Fresh Ways with Cakes:*
Editor: Gillian Moore
Researcher: Susie Dawson
Designer: Mary Staples
Sub-Editor: Wendy Gibbons

Editorial Production
Chief: Maureen Kelly
For the series:
Assistant: Deborah Fulham
Editorial Department: Theresa John, Debra Lelliott

U.S. Edition:
Assistant Editor: Barbara Fairchild Quarmby
Copy Coordinators: Mary Beth Oelkers-Keegan, Colette Stockum
Picture Coordinator: Betty Weatherly

Editorial Operations
Copy Chief: Diane Ullius
Production: Celia Beattie
Library: Louise D. Forstall

Correspondents: Elizabeth Kraemer-Singh (Bonn); Maria Vincenza Aloisi (Paris); Ann Natanson (Rome).

THE CONTRIBUTORS

ROSEMARY WADEY is an authority on home baking. She is a frequent contributor to cooking magazines and the author of many cookbooks, including *Delectable Cakes, Breads and Pastries, Biscuits and Cakes,* and *Cooking for Christmas.*

CAROL BOWEN, who has a degree in home economics, has specialized in creating recipes for the microwave oven. Her publications include *Complete Microwave Cookery* and *Microwave Cooking for One and Two.*

CAROLE HANDSLIP is a food writer and broadcaster with a particular interest in nutrition; the volumes she has written include *Wholefood Cookery* and *Vegetarian Cookery.* She has taught at the Cordon Bleu Cookery School in London.

JANICE MURFITT trained as a home economist and has worked as an editor for *Family Circle* magazine. Her primary interest now is developing recipes for cakes and pastries; her books include *Cake Icing and Decorating* and *Cheesecakes and Flans.*

JANE SUTHERING is a writer and home economist who has concentrated on desserts, cakes, and recipes using healthful foods. Her books include *Step-by-Step Cake Decorating.*

BARBARA SAUSE is an Arlington, Virginia, food writer and consultant who received a Grand Diplôme from Ecole de Cuisine La Varenne in Paris; she has written articles for *Cook's* and *Cooking Light* magazines, and has contributed to other volumes of Healthy Home Cooking.

THE COOKS
The recipes in this book were prepared for photographing by Pat Alburey, Allyson Birch, Carole Handslip, Janice Murfitt, Jane Suthering, and Rosemary Wadey.

THE CONSULTANT
PAT ALBUREY is a home economist with a wide experience in preparing foods for photography, teaching cooking, and creating recipes. She has written a number of cookbooks, including the *Harrods Book of Cakes and Desserts,* and she was the studio consultant for the Time-Life Books series The Good Cook. In addition to acting as the general consultant, she created a number of the recipes for this volume.

THE NUTRITION CONSULTANT
PATRICIA JUDD trained as a dietician and worked in hospital nutrition before returning to college to earn her MSc and PhD degrees. She has since lectured in Nutrition and Dietetics at London University.

Nutritional analyses for *Fresh Ways with Cakes* were derived from McCance and Widdowson's *The Composition of Food* by A. A. Paul and D. A. T. Southgate, and other current data.

Library of Congress Cataloging in Publication Data
Fresh ways with cakes.
   (Healthy home cooking)
   Includes index.
   1. Cake. I. Time-Life Books. II. Series
TX771.F735   1987   641.8'653   87-26774
ISBN 0-8094-6025-4
ISBN 0-8094-6026-2 (lib. bdg.)

For information on and a full description of any Time-Life Books series, please call 1-800-621-7026 or write:
Reader Information
Time-Life Customer Service
P.O. Box C-32068
Richmond, Virginia 23261-2068

Time-Life Books Inc. offers a wide range of fine recordings, including a *Rock 'n' Roll Era* series. For subscription information, call 1-800-621-7026, or write Time-Life Music, P.O. Box C-32068, Richmond, Virginia 23261-2068.

Other Publications:

AMERICAN COUNTRY
VOYAGE THROUGH THE UNIVERSE
THE THIRD REICH
THE TIME-LIFE GARDENER'S GUIDE
MYSTERIES OF THE UNKNOWN
TIME FRAME
FIX IT YOURSELF
FITNESS, HEALTH & NUTRITION
SUCCESSFUL PARENTING
UNDERSTANDING COMPUTERS
LIBRARY OF NATIONS
THE ENCHANTED WORLD
THE KODAK LIBRARY OF CREATIVE PHOTOGRAPHY
GREAT MEALS IN MINUTES
THE CIVIL WAR
PLANET EARTH
COLLECTOR'S LIBRARY OF THE CIVIL WAR
THE EPIC OF FLIGHT
THE GOOD COOK
WORLD WAR II
HOME REPAIR AND IMPROVEMENT
THE OLD WEST

This volume is one of a series of illustrated cookbooks that emphasize the preparation of healthful dishes for today's weight-conscious, nutrition-minded eaters.

Fresh Ways with Cakes

BY

THE EDITORS OF TIME-LIFE BOOKS

TIME-LIFE BOOKS / ALEXANDRIA, VIRGINIA

Contents

Caraway Sponge Cake

Poppy-Seed Twist

Semolina Fruit Cake

Black-Cherry Chocolate Gateau

Raspberry and Hazelnut Roulade

3 Small-Scale Delights....................94

4 Cakes from the Microwave..............126

Cherry-Walnut Yeast Cakes

The Pleasures of Baking

To many, cakes seem the epitome of nutritional frivolity—mere concentrated sugar and fat. Yet for those with a sweet tooth, life without the occasional feather-light sponge cake, moist fruit cake, or chocolate-covered morsel would be much the poorer. The 112 recipes in this volume are proof that cake can find a place in a healthful diet without overloading it with calories or sacrificing nutritional balance. A 2,000-calorie daily diet can accommodate both a 175-calorie dessert and a 250-calorie snack, either of which might consist of some home-baked delight. All but seven of the recipes presented on the following pages fall within the 250-calorie limit, and 47 of them fall within the 175-calorie limit. But health-conscious cooks are not simply calorie counting; they want each element of the diet to provide some positive benefit. Hence, the cakes in this volume also contribute to a person's daily intake of protein, dietary fiber, vitamins, and minerals.

Above all, the amount of fat—particularly saturated fat—is limited in these cakes. The slices of temptation that give cakes a bad name

are rich in butter, eggs, and nuts, and drowned in cream or chocolate. For a wholesome diet, all of these ingredients should be consumed in moderation, since dairy products, chocolate, and some nuts, notably coconut, are high in saturated fat, and egg yolks are the main source of cholesterol in the diet. A high level of cholesterol in the blood is strongly implicated in coronary artery disease, and the level of cholesterol is raised by eating large quantities of saturated fat. Some experts believe that a diet high in cholesterol also raises the amount of cholesterol in the blood.

Controlling saturated fat intake

Controlling the amount of saturated fat and cholesterol in these cakes has challenged the recipe-creators' ingenuity, for the ingredients high in these undesirable fats play an important structural role in cakes. Butter and eggs make cakes moist, palatable, and light: A classic technique for aerating cakes is to cream butter

with sugar until the blend is fluffy with captured air bubbles.

One way to cut down on saturated fat is to replace butter with fat that is less saturated; polyunsaturated fats have not been implicated in heart disease, and they actually appear to reduce blood cholesterol. The majority of the recipes in this volume call for polyunsaturated margarine rather than butter: Many margarines, particularly the hard ones, contain nearly as much saturated fat as butter, but most soft margarines are polyunsaturated. The recipes in this book that use oil specify safflower, the most polyunsaturated oil available; if it is impossible to find, however, you may substitute sunflower, which is the next best thing.

Many home-baking enthusiasts not only appreciate the advantages of margarine with regard to health, they actually prefer it to butter. Soft margarines require less working than butter and give lighter results. On the other hand, butter confers an incomparable flavor.

The balance of health, flavor, and texture can never be completely resolved; it depends on the recipe and on the eating habits of each person. Families that consume a good deal of cake would be wise to cut down on butter—but if a slice of cake is a very rare treat, you may prefer to consider flavor first. In most recipes, you can freely interchange margarine and butter, although a cake that calls for butter and contains a large amount of liquid may be too soft if polyunsaturated margarine is used. You cannot substitute oil for either butter or margarine, however: The difference in density produces different results and, unlike butter and margarine, oil will not incorporate air when it is beaten.

Butter has been limited in these cakes not only because of the risk of heart disease, but for the sake of the calorie count. Pound for pound, fat contains more than double the calories of carbohydrates or protein, so any modest reduction in the butter content of a recipe will sharply reduce calories. Substituting margarine or oil for butter does nothing for the calorie count of cakes, for margarine is as high in calories as butter, and oil is even higher. But the total fat content can be reduced by finding other ways of making the cake light and moist.

Fortunately, there are a number of alternatives to creamed butter or margarine for making a cake rise, all of which are explored in this volume. One is a combination of eggs and sugar whisked over heat to incorporate air: *Génoise,* the low-fat sponge cake leavened in this manner, is the foundation of many assembled creations in chapters 2 and 3. The *génoise* mixture does contain some saturated fat from egg yolks, but much less than a cake based on creamed butter. The *génoise* mixture is also high in cholesterol, but dietary cholesterol is probably of less nutritional concern than saturated fat, which raises blood cholesterol indirectly: Four eggs provide only 7 grams of saturated fat, whereas the same weight of butter provides 98 grams of saturated fat.

Another alternative to using creamed butter for leavening is to rely on yeast, a microscopic organism that produces carbon dioxide gas as a by-product of its metabolism. A third ploy is to use a chemical leavener, such as baking soda or powder. Baking soda is an alkali that releases carbon dioxide when moistened; it is most effective when an acid is present, and most cake recipes using baking soda include an acidic substance such as molasses, buttermilk, or even vinegar. Although baking powder works in a similar way, it contains its own acid and therefore does not need such additions. The majority of the recipes in this volume rely on a combination of leavening methods: a modest amount of creamed butter or margarine, for example, combined with a little baking powder.

Lacking large quantities of fat, the cakes would be dry if precautions were not taken. But the recipes solve the problem of dryness with many alternative moistening agents, ranging from fresh orange juice to zucchini, from tea to rum.

Novel sweeteners

Although limiting fat is the prime strategy for controlling the calorie count, limiting sugar also helps. Of course a cake needs sweetness—that is part of its attraction—but everyone can adjust to less sugar. This volume gently trains the palate in new ways, in some recipes by cutting down a little on the amount of sugar, in others by offering replacements for the white sugar traditionally poured into cakes. Sometimes the replacements provide extra flavor, sometimes fewer calories, and sometimes valuable nutrients in addition to fewer calories.

Many of the recipes use brown sugar instead of white; brown sugar—whether dark or light—has all the calories of white and negligible other nutrients, but its distinctive flavor makes a positive contribution to a cake and renders sweetness less important. One warning: Brown sugar, because of its moisture content, is often lumpy and needs sifting before mixing with other ingredients. Molasses, a by-product of sugar refining, has less sweetness, but even more flavor and a notable nutritional value: 1½ teaspoons of molasses—a reasonable helping incorporated into a slice of cake—contains about 15 percent of a person's daily iron requirement and about 5 percent of his or her calcium needs.

Many recipes in this volume use honey along with or instead of sugar, and a few recipes rely entirely on dried fruits for sweetness. Pound for pound, fructose, the sugar in fruit and honey, has the same number of calories as cane or beet sugar, but is one and a half times as sweet. Recipes that depend on honey, fruit, or powdered fructose for sweetness can thus contribute fewer calories while achieving the same degree of sweetness. Dried fruits provide iron and fiber in addition to their sweetness. Honey possesses virtually no nutritional edge over sugar, but it has a different advantage: It absorbs vapor from the air, so cakes become moister with time. Honey gives a heavier result than sugar, however, so it is not always suitable as a substitute.

The value of flour

Flour contributes a varying proportion—up to 50 percent in some recipes—of the calories in these cakes. Nutritionists consider flour a far better source of calories than sugar, because flour consists mainly of complex carbohydrates—chains of simple sugars that are digested more slowly than pure sugar, to satisfy hunger and provide energy for longer periods. Moreover, flour offers additional nutrients: About 10 percent of wheat flour is protein, and flour is also rich in iron and the B vitamins. White flour—milled from the inner layers of the wheat grain—contains a small amount of bran, which provides dietary fiber; whole wheat flour, milled from the entire grain, contains more than double the amount of bran. (When using whole wheat flour, note that, unlike all-purpose flour, it does not need sifting before combining with other ingredients: It never forms lumps in the bag. However, the best way to ensure the even distribution of a leavening agent or a spice throughout a cake is to sift it with the flour, whether or not the flour itself needs sifting.) Some manufacturers stress that their white flour is unbleached; in fact, most flour sold nowadays is unbleached, whether it says so or not. In this volume, all-purpose flour is the term used for unbleached white flour.

Recipes for cakes leavened with yeast often—though not always—specify bread flour; the high proportion of protein in bread flour forms a sturdy lattice that traps the bubbles of carbon dioxide very effectively. The result is a cake that is well risen and open-textured.

This volume does not subscribe to the view that whole wheat flour is invariably better than white. To be sure, it is richer in

The Key to Better Eating

Healthy Home Cooking addresses the concerns of weight- and health-conscious cooks with recipes that take into consideration guidelines that have been established by nutritionists. The secret to eating well, of course, has to do with maintaining a nutritional balance of foods in the diet. The recipes should therefore be used thoughtfully, in the context of a day's menu. To make the choice easier, this book offers an analysis of the nutrients in each recipe, as in the sample at right. In each case, the analysis applies to an individual serving. All of the figures that are given for calories, protein, cholesterol, total fat, saturated fat, and sodium are approximate ones.

Interpreting the chart

The chart below shows the National Research Council's Recommended Dietary Allowances of calories and protein for healthy men, women, and children, along with the council's recommendations for the "safe and adequate" maximum intake of sodium. Although the council has not established recommendations for either cholesterol or fat, the chart does include what the National Institutes of Health and the American Heart Association consider the daily maximum amounts of these for healthy members of the general population. The Heart Association, among other concerned groups, has pointed out that Americans derive about 40 percent of their calories from fat; this, it believes, should be cut back to less than 30 percent.

The volumes in the Healthy Home Cooking series do not purport to be diet books, nor do they focus on health foods. Instead, they express a commonsense approach to cooking that uses salt, sugar, cream, butter, and oil in moderation and employ other healthful ingredients that also provide flavor. In these cake recipes, spices, fruit, citrus zest, juices, wine and spirits, and vegetables are all used to achieve this end.

In this volume, a conscious effort has been made to limit the cakes to 250 calories per

Calories **178**
Protein **4g.**
Cholesterol **8mg.**
Total fat **4g.**
Saturated fat **1g.**
Sodium **15g.**

serving—the average comes to about 195—and to restrict the amount of total and saturated fats to 10 and 5 grams, respectively, per helping. Occasionally, in the interest of taste, texture, or even the successful cooking of a cake, the amount of sugar or fat has been increased. When a cake recipe exceeds the 250-calorie limit, the cook should cut back a little elsewhere in the daily menu.

The recipes make few unusual demands. Naturally, they call for fresh ingredients, offering substitutes when these are unavailable. (Only the original ingredient is calculated in the analysis, however.) Most of the items used in these cakes can be found in any well-stocked supermarket; any that may seem unfamiliar are described in a glossary on pages 140-141. To help the cook master new techniques, how-to photographs appear wherever appropriate.

About cooking times

Because the recipes emphasize fresh ingredients, they may take a little longer to prepare than dishes that call for packaged products. However, the rewards in flavor, and often in nutrition, should compensate for the extra time that is involved. To assist the cook in planning ahead, Healthy Home Cooking provides "working" and "total" times for each of the cakes.

Working time denotes the minutes actively spent on preparation; since no two cooks work at exactly the same speed, it is, of course, approximate. Any soaking or chilling specified in the recipe, as well as unattended cooking time, is calculated in the total time; again, because of the variations in ovens and cake pans, the cooking times should be considered only as an average. Total time also includes the minutes—or, more often, hours—that the cake requires in order to cool to room temperature. (Cooling times can vary by an hour or more, depending on the temperature of the kitchen.) A few of the cakes are not ready to slice even after they have cooled; any additional resting period needed to knit the cake's structure is thus included in total time.

Recommended Dietary Guidelines

| | | Average Daily Intake | | Maximum Daily Intake | | | |
		CALORIES	PROTEIN grams	CHOLESTEROL milligrams	TOTAL FAT grams	SATURATED FAT grams	SODIUM milligrams
Children	7-10	2400	22	240	80	27	1800
Females	11-14	2200	37	220	73	24	2700
	15-18	2100	44	210	70	23	2700
	19-22	2100	44	300	70	23	3300
	23-50	2000	44	300	67	22	3300
	51-75	1800	44	300	60	20	3300
Males	11-14	2700	36	270	90	30	2700
	15-18	2800	56	280	93	31	2700
	19-22	2900	56	300	97	32	3300
	23-50	2700	56	300	90	30	3300
	51-75	2400	56	300	80	27	3300

dietary fiber and some nutrients, and many people prefer its more robust flavor. For those reasons, it has won a prominent place in the book. On the other hand, however, whole wheat flour gives a heavier texture and a rougher appearance. For some cakes, it is simply not appropriate: Whole wheat madeleines would lose their delicacy, and whole wheat angel cake would be earthbound. In this volume, such flour has been used only in those recipes that benefit from it. If you wish to make judicious substitutions in other recipes, add an extra ½ teaspoon of baking powder per cup of whole wheat flour.

Embellishing the exterior

Hundreds of the calories in traditional cakes are found on the outside—in frostings, cream layers, butter icings. Cakes must look beautiful and festive, yet good looks need not mean dietary extravagance. This volume offers myriad decorating ideas that are low in calories and fat. Instead of a thick, solid layer, icing appears as a random dribble or a lattice of piped lines. Cream is often replaced with yogurt cheese or ricotta, which provide a real nutritional benefit in the form of protein and calcium. Hazelnut marzipan sometimes is used in place of the more fattening almond version. The jam specified for fillings is without added sugar; such jam is usually sweetened with concentrated apple juice. If you prefer, you can use reduced-sugar jam, which still offers a saving in calories.

Fruit, with its glowing colors and luscious contours, provides an endless source of decorative possibilities at minimal caloric expense. Because fresh fruit does not keep well once it is washed and sliced, you should always decorate with fruit at the last possible minute.

The majority of the recipes in the four chapters that follow are completely original. Some, however, are revised versions of traditional favorites. The rum babas on page 110, for example, made with a modest amount of butter and a light syrup, account for 175 calories and 2 grams of saturated fat each, while the standard version, laden with butter and sugar, provides in the neighborhood of 550 calories and 8 grams of saturated fat each. The Yule log on page 87, made from a chocolate-flavored batter filled with chestnuts, supplies only 175 calories and 2 grams of saturated fat per slice, whereas a slice of one that had been smothered in chocolate butter icing would have some 500 calories and 15 grams of saturated fat.

Like all cake recipes, the ones in this book rely on meticulous measurement and careful timing. A cake is not like a casserole, which can be varied according to the cook's whim with another splash of wine, a few more carrots. Substitutions are possible in cake recipes, but must be within limits that do not affect the consistency and rising capacity of the finished product. In some of the recipes, an editor's note offers successful alternatives.

Baking requires the cook to stay alert, since cooking times for cakes are affected by the temperature of the raw ingredients and the material of the pan. Cooking times can also vary widely from oven to oven. But if you have a convection oven, which circulates heat more quickly than a conventional one, it is usually better to retain the recommended cooking time and reduce the oven temperature by up to 100° F.; follow the manufacturer's guidelines scrupulously.

Although a few cakes, particularly the breadlike ones, are at their most delicious served warm, thorough cooling is as crucial for success with most cakes as is correctly judged cooking times. A cake cut before it has cooled completely develops a hard crust on the cut surface; a fruit cake cut while still warm will not be thoroughly bonded and may disintegrate. On a warm cake, icing will not set, and a cream or cheese topping will melt. Cooling times range from a few minutes for small cakes and 30 minutes for a sponge layer cake to approximately two hours for a large plain cake and four hours for a heavy fruit cake.

Many of the cakes in this volume are photographed with beverages, but the pictures are not intended to limit your choice of accompaniment. Provided it is not extremely sugary—and few of these cakes are—a cake served as a dessert may be enjoyed with a glass of sweet wine. To accompany a cake served as a midmorning or midafternoon snack, milk, coffee, and tea fill the bill admirably; fruit juices make a refreshing alternative and have the added benefit of vitamin C.

As a prelude to the recipes, some of the techniques and background knowledge that benefit the health-conscious baker are summarized. First of all, the chart on pages 10-11 provides key nutritional data on common cake ingredients. You can compare the nutritional profiles of, say, cream and yogurt, sugar and molasses, fresh and dried apricots. If you are thinking of substituting one type of nut for another or adding a garnish of fruit, you can calculate the consequences of the changes.

Pages 12-13 concentrate on basic skills—various ways of getting air into a batter and of lining cake pans. The following six pages offer a range of low-calorie finishing touches, from fruit purees to piped yogurt cheese and sugared rose petals. By allowing you to devise your own variations on the decorative ideas offered in the recipes, these techniques serve to multiply the number of healthful cakes you can create. All cakes—healthful ones included—are primarily for pleasure; with the skills that you learn in this volume, you will find the pleasures of creation rivaling those of consumption.

*Recommended daily intake

Dairy Products	*1900-2900 CALORIES	*47-72g. PROTEIN	*max. 300mg. CHOLESTEROL	*max. 72-109g. TOTAL FAT	*max. 32-48g. SATURATED FAT	*max. 2000mg. SODIUM
Skim milk (½ cup)	45	4	2	tr	2	65
Cottage cheese (1% fat) (½ cup)	80	14	5	1	1	460
Low-fat yogurt (½ cup)	75	6	7	2	1	80
Buttermilk (½ cup)	50	5	5	1	1	130
Whipping cream (½ cup)	410	3	163	44	27	45
Part-skim ricotta cheese (½ cup)	170	14	38	10	6	155
Fats and Eggs						
Unsalted butter (1 tbsp.)	100	tr	31	11	7.1	2
Polyunsaturated margarine (1 tbsp.)	100	tr	0	11	2	132
Safflower oil (1 tbsp.)	125	0	0	14	1.3	0
Egg (1 large)	80	6	272	6	1.7	69
Egg yolk	65	3	272	6	1.7	8
Egg white	15	3	0	tr	0	50

Fruits and Vegetables	*1900-2900 CALORIES	*47-72g. PROTEIN	*max. 300mg. CHOLESTEROL	*max. 72-109g. TOTAL FAT	*max. 32-48g. SATURATED FAT	*max. 2000mg. SODIUM
Apples (½ cup chopped)	35	tr	0	tr	.1	tr
Apricots (3 medium)	50	1	0	tr	tr	1
Bananas (2 medium)	210	2	0	2	.4	2
Figs, raw (3 medium)	110	1	0	1	tr	3
Grapes (½ lb.)	145	1	0	1	.2	5
Lemon (1 medium)	15	1	0	tr	tr	1
Orange (1 medium)	60	1	0	tr	tr	tr
Pineapple (1 cup chopped)	75	1	0	1	tr	2
Raspberries (1 cup whole)	60	1	0	1	tr	tr
Strawberries (1 cup whole)	45	1	0	1	tr	1
Apricots, dried (½ cup chopped)	155	3	0	1	tr	6
Dates, dried (½ cup chopped)	245	2	0	1	.2	3
Currants (½ cup)	205	3	0	tr	tr	6
Raisins (½ cup)	230	2	0	tr	.2	9
Carrots (½ cup grated)	25	1	0	tr	tr	20
Zucchini (½ cup grated)	10	1	0	tr	tr	1

The figures refer to the raw ingredient, the edible part only, fresh unless stated.

tr indicates that a trace is known to be present.

The figures given should be taken as a guide only; the composition of many foods can vary.

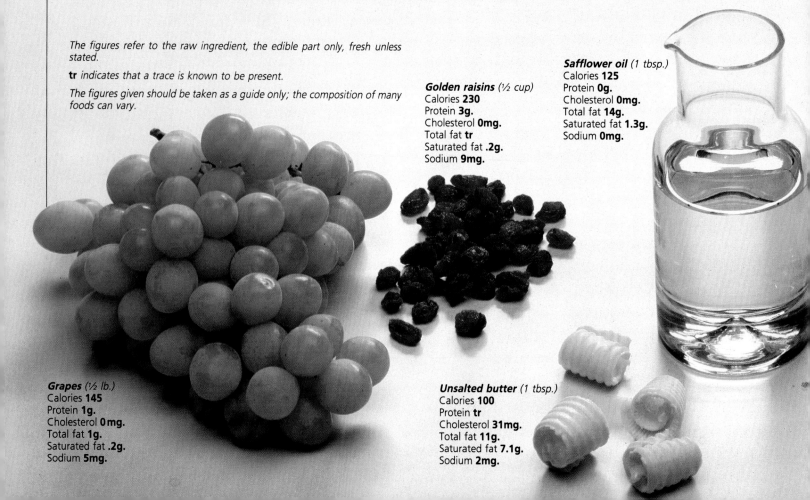

Golden raisins (½ cup)
Calories **230**
Protein **3g.**
Cholesterol **0mg.**
Total fat **tr**
Saturated fat **.2g.**
Sodium **9mg.**

Safflower oil (1 tbsp.)
Calories **125**
Protein **0g.**
Cholesterol **0mg.**
Total fat **14g.**
Saturated fat **1.3g.**
Sodium **0mg.**

Grapes (½ lb.)
Calories **145**
Protein **1g.**
Cholesterol **0mg.**
Total fat **1g.**
Saturated fat **.2g.**
Sodium **5mg.**

Unsalted butter (1 tbsp.)
Calories **100**
Protein **tr**
Cholesterol **31mg.**
Total fat **11g.**
Saturated fat **7.1g.**
Sodium **2mg.**

Nuts and Seeds

	*1900-2900 CALORIES	*47-72g. PROTEIN	*max. 300mg. CHOLESTEROL	*max. 72-109g. TOTAL FAT	*max. 32-48g. SATURATED FAT	*max. 2000mg. SODIUM
Almonds (½ cup whole)	455	14	0	41	3.8	8
Chestnuts (½ cup whole)	190	3	0	2	tr	2
Dried shredded coconut (1 tbsp.)	30	tr	0	2	1.9	14
Hazelnuts (½ cup whole)	420	9	0	42	3.0	2
Pecans (½ cup whole)	360	4	0	37	3.0	1
Pine nuts (½ cup whole)	345	6	0	36	5.8	43
Pistachio nuts (½ cup whole)	370	14	0	32	3.8	5
Walnuts (½ cup whole)	305	12	0	28	1.8	tr
Sesame seeds (1 tbsp.)	45	2	0	4	.6	3
Sunflower seeds (1 tbsp.)	50	2	0	5	.5	tr

Flours and Leavening Agents

	*1900-2900 CALORIES	*47-72g. PROTEIN	*max. 300mg. CHOLESTEROL	*max. 72-109g. TOTAL FAT	*max. 32-48g. SATURATED FAT	*max. 2000mg. SODIUM
All-purpose flour (1 cup)	420	12	0	1	.2	2
Whole wheat flour (1 cup)	400	16	0	2	.3	4
Rolled oats (1 cup)	310	13	0	5	.9	3
Baking powder (1 tsp.)	5	tr	0	0	0	405
Baking soda (1 tsp.)	0	0	0	0	0	820

Sweeteners and Flavorings

	*1900-2900 CALORIES	*47-72g. PROTEIN	*max. 300mg. CHOLESTEROL	*max. 72-109g. TOTAL FAT	*max. 32-48g. SATURATED FAT	*max. 2000mg. SODIUM
Sugar (½ cup)	385	0	0	0	0	5
Brown sugar (½ cup)	410	0	0	0	0	45
Fructose (1 tbsp.)	10	0	0	0	0	tr
Honey (1 tbsp.)	65	tr	0	0	0	1
Molasses (1 tbsp.)	45	0	0	0	0	14
Jam (without added sugar) (1 tbsp.)	6	0	0	0	0	0
Cocoa powder (1 tbsp.)	20	19	0	1	1	1
Semisweet chocolate (1 oz.)	143	1	0	10	6	4
Rum and brandy (1 tbsp.) (80 proof)	35	0	0	0	0	0

Nutrients in Cake Ingredients

Honey (1 tbsp.)
Calories **65**
Protein **tr**
Cholesterol **0mg.**
Total fat **0g.**
Saturated fat **0g.**
Sodium **1mg.**

Low-fat yogurt (½ cup)
Calories **75**
Protein **6g.**
Cholesterol **7mg.**
Total fat **2g.**
Saturated fat **1g.**
Sodium **80mg.**

Light brown sugar (½ cup)
Calories **410**
Protein **0g.**
Cholesterol **0mg.**
Total fat **0g.**
Saturated fat **0g.**
Sodium **45mg.**

Whipping cream (½ cup)
Calories **410**
Protein **3g.**
Cholesterol **163mg.**
Total fat **44g.**
Saturated fat **27g.**
Sodium **45mg.**

Airy Consistencies

One essential ingredient in virtually all cakes—although it does not show up in nutrient charts—is air. Three techniques for introducing air, and the consistency of the mixture to aim for, are described on this page.

When vigorously whisked, egg white captures air bubbles and puffs up to many times its original volume. Whether the egg white is to be folded into a cake batter or whisked with sugar to create meringue, it should be stiff enough to hold its shape *(left)*. Egg yolks or whole eggs whisked over heat with sugar enfold air and become the basis of a feather-light sponge cake. The whisking must continue until a trail of mixture falling from the whisk forms a glossy ribbon *(below, left)*. The airy foundation of numerous sponge and fruit cakes is butter or margarine, beaten with sugar until its color changes to the palest shade of cream *(below)*.

Stiffly Beaten Egg White

BEATING THE WHITES. Separate eggs carefully: Even a trace of yolk will hinder the whites from mounting. Put the whites in a large bowl—preferably one made of copper, which reacts chemically with the whites to strengthen the air bubbles. Using a balloon whisk, beat the whites in a figure-eight motion until they begin to foam. Changing to a circular action, whisk until the whites, when lifted on the whisk, hold a peak without the tip drooping.

Eggs and Sugar Beaten over Heat

1 *BEATING OVER HOT WATER. Place eggs and sugar in a large bowl and set it over a pan of simmering water. Beat with a whisk or an electric mixer for five to 10 minutes. The mixture will become thick and pale.*

2 *REACHING THE RIBBON STAGE. Remove the bowl from the heat. Continue to beat for five to 10 minutes, until the mixture is cool and falls from the whisk or beater to form a ribbon that lasts for at least 10 seconds.*

Butter and Sugar Beaten to a Cream

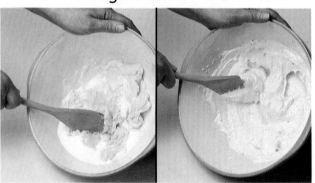

CREAMING WITH A WOODEN SPOON. Bring butter to room temperature; polyunsaturated margarine is softer and can be creamed while cool. Place margarine or—as here—butter in a large mixing bowl. Hold the bowl at an angle and use a wooden spoon or an electric mixer to beat the margarine or butter until it is soft (above, left). Beat in sugar—here, an equal proportion is used. Continue to beat until the mixture is fluffy and virtually white.

Lining Pans
for Flawless Results

Disk for a Shallow Pan

DUSTING WITH FLOUR. Brush the pan with oil or melted margarine. Cut a circle of paper to fit the base of the pan and press it into place. For wax paper (above), brush the paper with oil or melted margarine, spoon in a little flour, and rotate the pan to distribute it. Tip the pan to remove the excess.

Two Layers for a Deep Pan

LINING THE SIDES. Cut two disks of nonstick parchment paper to fit the base. Cut two strips for the sides, adding an extra 2 inches in height. Fold a 1-inch hem and snip it. Grease the inside of the pan. Insert one disk, then the side strips. Grease the first disk, then add the second.

Molds for small cakes need no more preparation than a film of butter or margarine and a dusting of flour: The flour browns to give the cake a light crust. But pans for large cakes must be lined with paper to help the baked cake slip out without breaking.

This page shows how to prepare linings for a shallow cake pan (far left), a deep, round cake pan (left), and a rectangular pan (below). For a shallow pan, whether round or rectangular, a base lining is adequate. To help turn out a deep cake, the sides of the pan must be lined as well as the bottom. For a long-cooking cake, such as a fruit cake, the double lining shown on the deep, round pan will prevent scorching.

Parchment paper that has a silicone coating to prevent sticking is the best material for lining pans. In place of parchment paper, use well-greased wax paper. Parchment paper does not usually need greasing, although a light coating of fat is recommended in a few recipes for mixtures that are likely to stick.

A Tailored Lining for a Rectangular Pan

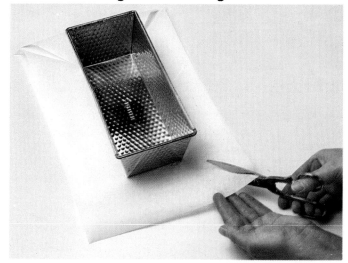

1 CUTTING NEAT CORNERS. Cut a sheet of parchment paper large enough to cover the bottom and sides of the pan. Place the pan in the center of the sheet. Cut a straight diagonal line from each corner of the paper to the nearest corner of the pan (above).

2 FITTING THE PAPER. Grease the inside of the pan with oil or melted margarine. Insert the paper into the pan, and press it firmly against the bottom and sides. Overlap the corner flaps, lightly greasing the undersides so that the pairs of flaps adhere and lie flat.

Techniques for Preparing Fruit

The rich colors and fresh flavors of fruits, together with their low calorie content and total lack of fat, make them invaluable for filling and decorating healthful cakes.

Some fruits, such as strawberries, can be used just as they are, but citrus fruits must be rid of the peel and all of the pith *(box, right)*; soft fruits such as peaches and apricots need light cooking to loosen the skins and to further soften them *(box, below right)*.

For filling or topping sponge cakes, lemon curd or fresh fruit purees thickened with arrowroot *(opposite page)* make perfect alternatives to jam. In the box below appear two pureeing methods, suitable for soft and firm fruits, respectively. Apples and pears, however, should be peeled, sliced, and cooked gently in a heavy-bottomed saucepan with a few tablespoons of water and a little sugar—about 1/3 cup per 1 lb. of fruit—until they become soft and fluffy. After draining in a nylon sieve to remove excess juice, the resulting puree does not need to be thickened.

Segmenting an Orange

1 REMOVING THE PEEL. Using a sharp knife, slice off the peel at both ends of the orange. Stand the fruit on a flat end and slice downward to remove all of the peel in vertical strips. This technique of cutting away zest and pith together ensures that every trace of pith is removed.

2 CUTTING OUT THE SEGMENTS. Working over a bowl to catch the juice, hold the orange in one hand, and slice between flesh and membrane to remove each of the segments. The orange segments will now make a fresh and appealing cake decoration.

Two Ways of Pureeing

SIEVING SOFT FRUITS. To puree raspberries, blackberries, or—as here—strawberries, put the fruit in a nylon sieve set over a bowl. Using a wooden pestle, push the fruit through the sieve. Before putting apricots, peaches, and plums through a sieve, cook for a few minutes in a heavy-bottomed saucepan with a little sugar—1/4 to 1/2 cup per lb. of fruit.

BLENDING FIRM FRUITS. Puree firm fruit such as mango, papaya, or—as here—pineapple in a blender or food processor. Peel and core the pineapple and cut the flesh into chunks. Put the pineapple in a food processor or blender, and process the fruit in short bursts.

Removing Skins

POACHING AND SKINNING. Halve and pit plums or—as here—apricots. Simmer them in water until tender—three to seven minutes. Drain the apricots on a drum sieve or a rack, and pull off the skins. With peaches and nectarines, immerse the whole fruit in boiling water for two minutes. Drain, skin, halve, and pit the fruit. Poach it until tender—five to 15 minutes.

Thickened Fruit Puree

WITH THE EXCEPTION OF APPLE PUREE, MOST FRUIT PUREES
NEED TO BE THICKENED BEFORE THEY CAN BE USED
AS CAKE FILLINGS OR TOPPINGS SO THAT THEY DO NOT
OOZE OUT OR RUN OFF THE FINISHED CAKE.
WHEN THICKENED WITH ARROWROOT, THEY BECOME CLEAR
AND SPARKLING, WITH SOFT, JELLYLIKE CONSISTENCY.

Makes 1 cup
Working time: about 10 minutes
Total time: about 1 hour and 30 minutes

1 cup fresh fruit puree (opposite)
1 tbsp. arrowroot
2 tbsp. sugar

Put the fruit puree in a small saucepan. Blend the arrowroot with 1 tablespoon of cold water, then stir it into the puree. Bring the mixture to a boil, stirring constantly; boil until it thickens and clears. Continue to cook the puree over low heat for three to four minutes, until there is no trace of any uncooked arrowroot. Stir in the sugar. Pour the puree into a small bowl and place plastic wrap directly on top of the puree, to prevent a skin from forming. Allow the thickened puree to cool, then refrigerate it until it is set and thoroughly chilled.

EDITOR'S NOTE: *About ½ lb. of prepared fresh fruit will yield 1 cup of puree.*

Lemon Curd

Makes 1 lb.
Working time: about 40 minutes
Total time: about 4 hours

2 lemons, zest finely grated, juice squeezed and strained
6 tbsp. polyunsaturated margarine
⅔ cup sugar
3 eggs, lightly beaten

Put the lemon zest, juice, margarine, and sugar in a mixing bowl. Strain the eggs through a sieve into the bowl. Place the bowl over a saucepan of gently simmering water, making sure that the bottom of the bowl does not touch the water. Stir the mixture continuously over the heat *(Step 2, below)* until it becomes thick enough to leave a trail when the spoon is lifted— 20 to 25 minutes. Alternatively, put the bowl in a microwave oven and cook the curd on high for three minutes, stirring every 30 seconds with a wire whisk.

As soon as the mixture thickens, transfer it to a clean, warm jar. Allow the lemon curd to cool, then refrigerate it. When it is cold, cover the jar with a clean lid or plastic wrap secured with a rubber band. Keep the jar refrigerated and use the curd within two weeks.

Making Lemon Curd

1 COMBINING THE INGREDIENTS. Put sugar in a bowl with margarine, lemon zest, and juice (recipe above). Lightly whisk eggs in another bowl. Add the eggs to the other ingredients, pouring them through a nylon sieve to remove any white threads.

2 THICKENING THE CURD. Set the bowl over a pan of gently simmering water. So that the eggs do not cook too quickly and coagulate in lumps, make sure that the bottom of the bowl does not touch the water. Cook the curd, stirring constantly, for about 20 to 25 minutes.

3 STORING THE CURD. When the curd begins to thicken and will fall from a spoon in a ribbon, warm a clean glass jar to prevent it from cracking, then spoon in the curd and let it cool completely. (It will thicken further as it cools.) Cover and store in the refrigerator.

Pastry Cream Variations

PASTRY CREAM OR *CRÈME PÂTISSIÈRE* IS A CUSTARD USED FOR FILLING AND DECORATING CAKES; IT IS TRADITIONALLY ENRICHED WITH NUMEROUS EGG YOLKS AND THICKENED WITH FLOUR. THIS VERSION IS ENRICHED ONLY WITH A LITTLE YOGURT; IN THE ABSENCE OF EGG YOLKS, CORNSTARCH IS EASIER TO BLEND WITH THE OTHER INGREDIENTS; IT THEREFORE REPLACES THE FLOUR. THE EGG WHITE LIGHTENS THE MIXTURE, BUT IT IS NOT ESSENTIAL. THE BASIC PASTRY CREAM RECIPE CAN BE ENLIVENED BY ADDING A VARIETY OF FLAVORINGS.

Makes about 2 cups
Working time: about 20 minutes
Total time: about 4 hours

½ cup cornstarch
⅓ cup sugar
2⅓ cups skim milk
1 tsp. pure vanilla extract
1 egg white (optional)
¼ cup plain low-fat yogurt

Blend the cornstarch in a bowl with the sugar and ⅓ cup of the milk. Heat the remaining milk in a saucepan and bring it to a boil. Pour the boiling milk over the blended cornstarch, stirring constantly. Pour the mixture back into the saucepan and cook over low heat, whisking at first and then stirring, for six to eight minutes, until every trace of raw cornstarch is gone. Beat in the vanilla extract. Strain the custard through a nylon sieve into a clean bowl and place plastic wrap directly on the custard, to prevent a skin from forming. Allow the pastry cream to cool, then refrigerate it for two to three hours, or overnight, until it is cold.

Whisk the cold custard until it is very smooth. Beat the egg white until it forms soft peaks. Fold the yogurt into the custard, then gradually fold in the egg white. Cover the bowl and return the pastry cream to the refrigerator to chill thoroughly.

Liqueur-flavored pastry cream. Stir 4 tablespoons of brandy, rum, or a liqueur such as kirsch into the custard along with the vanilla extract.

Orange-flavored pastry cream. Add the grated zest of two oranges to the cold milk in the saucepan. In place of the vanilla extract, add 2 tablespoons of Grand Marnier.

Coffee-flavored pastry cream. Stir 2 tablespoons of very strong black coffee into the custard with the vanilla extract.

Chocolate-flavored pastry cream. Add 2 tablespoons of cocoa powder to the initial blend of cornstarch, sugar, and milk.

Almond pastry cream. Add ½ cup of ground almonds and 3 drops of almond extract to the custard at the same time as the yogurt.

Essential Piping Skills

An edge of piped shells or a lattice of piped lines adds a polished finish to an otherwise simple cake. Piping makes small amounts of topping go further, so it is often used in this volume for distributing cream, glacé icing, and chocolate. You can also pipe yogurt cheese *(Glossary, page 140)* and a low-calorie adaptation of classic pastry cream *(box, left)*. When piped, yogurt cheese gives crisp outlines; pastry cream, especially when lightened with egg white, has softer contours.

Dribbling fine lines of icing or chocolate is best accomplished with a homemade wax or parchment paper pastry bag *(far right)*. For piping cream, pastry cream, or soft cheese, use a nylon bag fitted with a tip—a star tip is the most versatile. The photographs on the right show how to fill a pastry bag correctly, and below are three designs that you can achieve with the star tip. If you have not piped before, it is best to practice on a work surface or an upturned plate before decorating the cake.

Three Basic Patterns

Fit a pastry bag with a medium-size star tip and fill the bag (above, right): Here, yogurt cheese is used. Grasp the bag with one hand at the top to squeeze, and the other hand near the nozzle to control it. To pipe stars, hold the bag at a perpendicular angle, with the tip just above the work surface. Squeeze the bag gently; when the star reaches the desired size, stop squeezing and lift the bag away sharply. To pipe a straight line, hold the bag at an angle just above the work surface. Pipe toward yourself, keeping an even pressure. To finish, lower the tip and pull the bag sharply to one side. To pipe shells, hold the bag at an angle, close to the work surface. Squeeze a small mound, then raise the bag. Reduce the pressure; lower the bag as you bring it toward you. Repeat to create a series of overlapping shells.

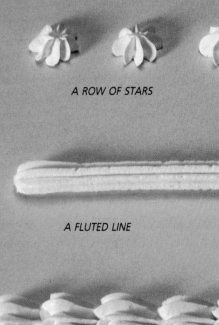

A ROW OF STARS

A FLUTED LINE

A STRING OF SHELLS

Making a Paper Pastry Bag

Preparing to Pipe

1 FILLING THE BAG. Push a tip into position in a pastry bag. Fold the top back and hold it by the collar thus formed. Fill it only three-quarters full—here, pastry cream is used.

2 EXCLUDING AIR. Supporting the bag loosely with one hand, twist the top of the bag with the other. This action will squeeze out any air pockets; the bag is now ready for piping.

1 FORMING A CONE. Cut a square from a sheet of wax or parchment paper, then cut the square in half diagonally. Using only one triangle, bring one corner of the long side to meet the right-angle corner, bending the first corner over to form a cone.

2 COMPLETING THE CONE. Keeping the first cone in position, curl the remaining side around it, in the same way as above. Holding the corners in both hands, adjust them to create a perfect point at the tip of the cone.

3 SECURING THE BAG. Fold the corners over to prevent the cone from coming apart. Snip a hole in the tip through which to dribble icing or chocolate. The size of the hole will determine the thickness of the piping.

Decorative Ideas

Some of the prettiest cake decorations are simple to create and low in calories. Citrus zest, cut into julienne strips *(right)*, lends color and contrast. A sugar frosting transforms grapes or edible flower petals *(far right)* into sparkling jewels. Chocolate is high in fat and calories, but chocolate curls and leaves *(opposite page)* make the most of small quantities; a chocolate leaf has only 18 calories.

A sprinkling of confectioners' sugar finishes a cake attractively and adds only five to 10 calories per slice. To create a pattern, you can mask part of the cake with paper doilies, cardboard shapes, or strips of wax paper before sifting the sugar over it *(below)*. You can also brand the sugar with a red-hot skewer *(below, right)* to create caramelized stripes.

Julienne Strips

PARING AND BLANCHING. Pare thin layers of zest in long strips from an orange, a lime, or—as here—a lemon. Scrape any white pith from the zest, and trim the ragged edges. Cut the zest into narrow strips (above). Parboil the strips for three minutes; drain them and pat them dry.

Sugar-Frosted Petals

APPLYING A COATING. Beat an egg white until it lightens without foaming. Brush violets, primroses, geraniums, or—as here— rose petals with it, then dip them in sugar. Transfer the petals to a plate and leave them in a warm place until dry and hard. In an airtight container, they will keep for weeks.

Stencil Patterns with Confectioners' Sugar

MASKING AREAS OF THE CAKE. Cut strips of wax paper, each about ½-inch wide and slightly longer than the diameter of the cake. Lay them on top of the cake and sift confectioners' sugar evenly over the surface. Lift away each strip carefully, to avoid smearing the sugar.

Heat-Branded Confectioners' Sugar

APPLYING A RED-HOT SKEWER. Sift a thick, even layer of confectioners' sugar over the cake. Heat a long skewer in a flame or on an electric burner, protecting your hand with a cloth if the skewer lacks a wooden handle. When the skewer is red-hot, brand the cake with parallel lines or a grid pattern; reheat the skewer if necessary.

Chocolate Curls

SCRAPING THE BLOCK. Choose soft chocolate for long curls; hard chocolate produces shorter curls. The chocolate must be at room temperature, otherwise it may not curl. Hold the block over a plate and draw a vegetable peeler along the thin edge, allowing the shavings to curl and fall free.

Chocolate Rose Leaves

1 *COATING A LEAF. Wipe small rose leaves with a towel. Break a chocolate bar into small, even pieces: 2½ oz. yields 20 leaves. Put the chocolate on a plate and set it over a pan of simmering water until it melts. Remove the plate from the heat. Holding each leaf by its stem, gently press the underside against the chocolate. Pull the leaf across the side of the plate to remove the excess.*

2 *PEELING AWAY A LEAF. Transfer the leaves, chocolate side up, to a clean plate. Leave them in a cool place—but not in the refrigerator—until the coating is hard. Starting at the stem (above), carefully peel each leaf away from the chocolate.*

1 Candied peel, golden raisins, molasses, and other ingredients for a moist, dark fruit cake await the cook's attentions.

Simple Sponge and Fruit Cakes

Cakes for everyday enjoyment should beguile the eye and palate without requiring elaborate assembly or intricate decoration. The cakes in this chapter will grace a family meal, honor an unexpected caller, or satisfy a bevy of hungry children—and although they may take several hours to bake and cool, few demand more than 30 minutes of the cook's active efforts. Ranging from a frosted orange sponge cake to a moist, fruit-packed Dundee cake, the recipes cater to every taste.

The airiest cakes of all, the angel food cakes, might have been invented with the health-conscious cook in mind. Lacking all fat, angel food cake is raised to prodigious heights with stiffly beaten egg whites alone. Other sponge cakes, by contrast, are aerated chiefly with fat and sugar that have been creamed to virtual whiteness. The classic sponge cake consists of eggs, flour, sugar, and butter or margarine, as well as flavorings such as chocolate, sherry, or orange zest; in these recipes, the fat is reduced and baking powder is usually added to help leaven the cake.

Dense and dark, the dried fruit and nut cakes on pages 42 to 54 offer a striking contrast to the feather-light sponge cakes. Some of the dried fruit and nut cakes, like the sponge cakes, are raised partly with creamed fat. But a number are fat-free mixtures that are leavened with baking powder alone; others include small amounts of butter rubbed into the flour with the fingers. Variety comes not just from different mixtures of berries, tropical fruit, candied peel, and nuts, but from a range of flour types, including whole wheat flour, dark rye flour, and protein-rich soy flour.

The spice, fresh fruit cakes, and vegetable cakes that make up the rest of this chapter are no less diverse. For flavor and moisture, they employ a range of surprising ingredients, from saffron to pineapple and zucchini.

Step-by-step photographs in the chapter offer guidance for special techniques, such as creating the poppy seed braid shown on pages 38 and 39. For basic cake-making and decorating methods, including creaming butter and lining pans, pages 12 to 19 provide more detail than the individual recipes.

Sponge Cake Variations

Serves 12
Working time: about 20 minutes
Total time: about 1 hour and 30 minutes

Plain sponge cake with jam filling:

Calories **190**
Protein **3g.**
Cholesterol **45mg.**
Total fat **9g.**
Saturated fat **3g.**
Sodium **140mg.**

½ cup polyunsaturated margarine
⅔ cup sugar
1¼ cups all-purpose flour
1½ tsp. baking powder
2 eggs
4 tsp. fresh lemon juice
3 tbsp. raspberry, strawberry, or apricot jam without added sugar

Whole wheat sponge cake with jam and cheese filling:

Calories **185**
Protein **3g.**
Cholesterol **45mg.**
Total fat **9g.**
Saturated fat **3g.**
Sodium **160mg.**

Chocolate sponge cake with yogurt cheese filling:

Calories **180**
Protein **3g.**
Cholesterol **45mg.**
Total fat **9g.**
Saturated fat **3g.**
Sodium **135mg.**

Preheat the oven to 375° F. Grease two 8-inch round cake pans. Line the bottoms with parchment or wax paper; grease the paper. Dredge the pans with flour and shake out the excess.

Cream the margarine with all but 2 tablespoons of the sugar in a large bowl until the mixture is very pale and fluffy. Sift the flour and baking powder together into another bowl. Using a wooden spoon, beat one egg at a time into the sugar mixture, following each with 1 tablespoon of the flour. Mix in the remaining flour and the lemon juice. Divide the mixture between the two prepared pans and level the surfaces.

Bake the sponge cakes for 20 to 25 minutes, until well risen, golden brown, and just firm to the touch. Turn them out onto a wire rack, and leave the paper attached until they have cooled completely.

Strip off the paper. Place one sponge layer on a plate, and spread it with jam. Set the second layer on top of the first and then sift the remaining sugar evenly over the top of the cake.

Variations

1. For a richer flavor and a moister texture, make the sponge cake with light brown sugar instead of granulated sugar.

2. For a whole-wheat sponge cake, replace half the flour with whole wheat flour and increase the baking powder by ¼ teaspoon.

3. For a lemon sponge cake, add the grated zest of one lemon.

4. For a chocolate sponge cake, replace 2 tablespoons of the flour with sifted cocoa powder and use water in place of the lemon juice.

5. For a richer filling, beat 2 tablespoons of low-fat ricotta cheese into the jam.

6. Replace the jam filling with a thickened fruit puree *(page 15);* lemon curd *(page 15);* flavored pastry cream *(page 16);* or 4 tablespoons of yogurt cheese *(Glossary, page 140),* sweetened with 1 tablespoon of confectioners' sugar.

7. Sift 2 tablespoons of confectioners' sugar over the cake in place of the granulated sugar. Alternatively, lay a doily on the sponge cake, and sift ¼ cup of confectioners' sugar over it. Carefully remove the doily to reveal a pattern on the cake.

Clockwise from top: plain sponge cake with jam filling and granulated sugar topping; whole-wheat sponge cake with jam and cheese filling and confectioners' sugar topping; chocolate sponge cake with yogurt cheese filling and confectioners' sugar topping.

Frosted Orange Cake

Serves 14
Working time: about 25 minutes
Total time: about 3 hours and 30 minutes

Calories **220**
Protein **3g.**
Cholesterol **30mg.**
Total fat **7g.**
Saturated fat **2g.**
Sodium **100mg.**

| 2⅓ cups all-purpose flour |
| 2½ tsp. baking powder |
| ½ cup polyunsaturated margarine |
| ⅓ cup light brown sugar |
| 2 oranges, grated zest only |
| 2 eggs |
| 1 cup fresh orange juice |
| **Orange glacé icing** |
| 1 cup confectioners' sugar |
| 3 tsp. fresh orange juice |
| ½ orange, grated zest only |

Preheat the oven to 325° F. Line a deep 7- or 8-inch round pan with parchment paper.

Sift the flour and baking powder together into a bowl and, using your fingertips or the back of a wooden spoon, rub in the margarine until the mixture resembles fine bread crumbs. Stir in the brown sugar and orange zest. In another bowl, beat the eggs and orange juice together, and then mix them into the dry ingredients with a wooden spoon. Pour the batter into the prepared pan and level the top. Bake the cake for about one hour, until well risen and firm to the touch; a skewer inserted in the center of the cake should come out clean. Turn the cake out onto a wire rack, allow it to cool, and then peel off the paper.

To make the icing, sift the confectioners' sugar into a bowl and beat in just enough of the orange juice to give a thick consistency. Ice the top of the cake, allowing the icing to run down the sides. Sprinkle with the grated orange zest and let the icing set.

Coffee Layer Cake

Serves 12
Working time: about 30 minutes
Total time: about 2 hours and 15 minutes

Calories **190**
Protein **3g.**
Cholesterol **45mg.**
Total fat **9g.**
Saturated fat **3g.**
Sodium **160mg.**

½ cup polyunsaturated margarine
⅔ light brown sugar
2 eggs
½ cup whole wheat flour
1 cup all-purpose flour
1¾ tsp. baking powder
1 tbsp. molasses
1 tbsp. very strong black coffee
⅔ cup coffee-flavored pastry cream (page 16)
2 tbsp. confectioners' sugar

Preheat the oven to 375° F. Grease two 8-inch round cake pans and line the bottoms with parchment paper.

Cream the margarine and brown sugar together in a bowl until they are pale and fluffy. With a wooden spoon, beat in the eggs one at a time, following each with 1 tablespoon of the whole wheat flour. Sift the all-purpose flour with the baking powder and mix it with the remaining whole wheat flour; then add the flour to the creamed mixture, alternating it with the molasses and coffee. Divide the batter between the prepared pans and level the tops. Bake the cakes for 20 to 25 minutes, until well risen and firm to the touch. Turn them out onto a wire rack, allow them to cool completely, and then peel off the paper.

To assemble the cake, place one layer on a serving plate and spread the coffee-flavored pastry cream evenly over it. Cover it with the second layer, then sift the confectioners' sugar over the cake. Heat a skewer until it is red hot and use it to brand a lattice pattern on the cake *(page 18)*. To soften the contrast between these marks and the rest of the surface, complete the decoration with a second, very light dusting of confectioners' sugar.

Chiffon Cake with Raspberry-Cream Filling

CHIFFON CAKE OBTAINS A THREEFOLD LEAVENING FROM BEATEN EGG WHITES, BAKING POWDER, AND THE STEAM ESCAPING FROM A MOIST BATTER. OIL IS TRADITIONALLY USED IN THE MIXTURE; THIS RECIPE KEEPS THE PROPORTION VERY LOW.

Serves 16
Working time: about 35 minutes
Total time: about 1 hour and 20 minutes

Calories **210**
Protein **3g.**
Cholesterol **45mg.**
Total fat **9g.**
Saturated fat **2g.**
Sodium **110mg.**

1⅓ cups all-purpose flour
3 tsp. baking powder
⅔ cup sugar, plus 1 tbsp.
3 tbsp. safflower oil
3 egg yolks
6 egg whites

Fruit and cream filling
⅓ cup sugar
4 fresh peaches, sliced
2 tbsp. brandy
1 cup whipping cream
1 cup fresh raspberries

Preheat the oven to 325° F. Grease two 8½-inch round cake pans. Line the bottoms with wax paper and grease the paper.

Sift the flour and baking powder into a bowl and mix in the ⅔ cup of sugar. Make a well in the center. In another bowl, whisk the oil and egg yolks with 5 tablespoons of water until well blended. In a third bowl, whisk the egg whites until they are stiff but not dry. Pour the egg-yolk mixture into the dry ingredients and beat with a wooden spoon to create a smooth, glossy batter. Add one-third of the egg whites to the batter and fold them in using a spatula or large spoon. Then carefully fold in the remaining whites.

Divide the mixture equally between the two prepared pans, and tap them to level the mixture. Bake the cakes in the center of the oven until they are well risen, lightly browned, and springy when touched in the center—about 20 minutes. Loosen the edges of the cakes with a knife, turn them out of the pans onto a wire rack, and remove the lining paper. Allow the cakes to cool completely.

Meanwhile, prepare the filling. Put all but 1 tablespoon of the sugar and ⅔ cup of water in a wide, shallow saucepan. Heat gently, stirring, until the sugar dissolves, then bring to a boil. Boil the syrup gently for four to five minutes to reduce it slightly. Simmer the peach slices in the syrup for one to two minutes, until they begin to soften. Using a slotted spoon, transfer the slices to a paper towel to drain. Peel the slices. Stir 1 tablespoon of brandy into the syrup. Whip the cream with the remaining tablespoon of sugar and the remaining brandy until the cream will hold soft peaks.

Set one of the cake layers on a serving plate. Spoon half of the brandy syrup evenly over the cake, then spread the cake with half of the whipped cream. Arrange the peach slices and raspberries on the cream. Spread the remaining cream over the fruit.

Leaving the other cake upside down on the rack, spoon the remaining brandy syrup over it. Invert the cake and set it on the first layer. Sift the tablespoon of sugar over the cake.

EDITOR'S NOTE: *To make a chocolate chiffon cake, replace 4 tablespoons of the flour with cocoa powder.*

Streusel Ring

Serves 16
Working time: about 25 minutes
Total time: about 3 hours and 30 minutes

Calories **230**
Protein **3g.**
Cholesterol **35mg.**
Total fat **10g.**
Saturated fat **4g.**
Sodium **145 mg.**

2⅓ cups all-purpose flour
2½ tsp. baking powder
½ cup polyunsaturated margarine
½ cup dried shredded coconut
⅓ cup light brown sugar
2 limes, grated zest only
2 eggs
2 tbsp. honey
4 tbsp. skim milk
Coconut streusel topping
½ cup whole wheat flour
2 tbsp. polyunsaturated margarine
2 tbsp. light brown sugar
1 tbsp. dried shredded coconut

Preheat the oven to 350° F. Thoroughly grease a tubular springform pan about 9 inches in diameter.

Sift the flour and baking powder into a bowl and, using your fingertips or the back of a wooden spoon, rub in the margarine until the mixture resembles fine bread crumbs. Mix in the coconut, sugar, and lime zest. Put the eggs, honey, and milk in a small bowl and whisk them together, then beat them into the flour and margarine mixture with a wooden spoon. Turn the batter into the prepared pan and level the top.

To make the streusel topping, put the flour into a bowl and rub in the margarine. Mix in the sugar and coconut. Sprinkle the blend evenly over the top of the batter. Cook the streusel ring for about one hour, until well risen and firm; a skewer inserted in the center should come out clean. Leave the cake in the pan for five minutes, then release the spring and turn the cake out carefully onto a wire rack to cool.

Pistachio Battenburg Cake

PISTACHIOS REPLACE ALMONDS TO GIVE A MARZIPAN WITH AN
UNUSUAL FLAVOR AND A NATURAL GREEN COLOR.

Serves 16
Working time: about 1 hour
Total time: about 14 hours

Calories **250**
Protein **3g.**
Cholesterol **30mg.**
Total fat **12g.**
Saturated fat **2g.**
Sodium **180mg.**

½ cup polyunsaturated margarine
⅔ cup light brown sugar
2 eggs
1⅓ cups all-purpose flour
1½ tsp. baking powder
2 tsp. strong black coffee
1 tsp. cocoa powder
3 tbsp. apricot jam without added sugar
Pistachio marzipan
1 cup pistachio nuts
½ cup sugar
⅔ cup confectioners' sugar
1 tsp. fresh lemon juice
1 egg white, lightly beaten

For the pistachio marzipan, blanch the pistachio nuts
for two minutes in simmering water. Drain them, wrap
them in a towel, and rub them to loosen their skins.
Peel the kernels. Spread them out on paper towels for
several hours to dry in a warm place.

Preheat the oven to 350° F. Line a rectangular pan
approximately 7 by 11 by 1½ inches with parchment
paper, making a deep pleat in the center to divide the
pan crosswise into two portions.

Using a wooden spoon, cream the margarine and
brown sugar together in a large bowl until the mixture
is very pale and fluffy. Beat in the eggs one at a time,
following each with 1 tablespoon of the flour. Sift the
remaining flour and the baking powder together into
the mixture, and fold them in.

Transfer one-half of the mixture to a second bowl.
Into one portion beat the coffee; into the other, beat
the cocoa powder and 2 teaspoons of water. Spoon
the coffee mixture into one side of the prepared pan
and the chocolate mixture into the other side. Bake the
cakes for 20 to 25 minutes, until they are firm to the
touch. Turn them out onto a rack, remove the lining
paper, and let them cool.

Using a rotary grater or a food processor, grind the
pistachios finely into a bowl. Add the granulated sugar
and sift in the confectioners' sugar. Mix in the lemon
juice and enough of the egg white to give a firm but
pliable consistency.

Trim the cakes to the same size and cut each in half
lengthwise. Spread the side of one chocolate section
lightly with jam and press one of the coffee sections
against it. Join the other two with jam in the same way.
Spread jam over the top of one pair of cakes. Press the
second pair down on the first, making sure that a
coffee section is over a chocolate section, and a chocolate section over a coffee section, so that the finished
cake will have a checkerboard pattern when it is sliced.

Dust the pistachio marzipan with a little confectioners' sugar and roll it out between two sheets of parchment paper. Remove the top sheet and trim the marzipan into a rectangle just large enough to enclose the
cake—about 9 by 12 inches. Spread all four sides of
the cake very lightly with jam and position it in the
center of the marzipan. Wrap the marzipan evenly
around the cake, peeling back the parchment paper.
Press the edges of the marzipan together so that they
adhere (they are very sticky) and trim off the ends.

Stand the cake on a serving plate and score the top
of the cake with a sharp knife to give a crisscross
pattern. Pinch the top edges with a finger and thumb.
Leave the cake uncovered overnight; it will become dry
enough to slice.

Chocolate Marble Cake

Serves 20
Working time: about 20 minutes
Total time: about 3 hours

Calories **215**
Protein **3g.**
Cholesterol **60mg.**
Total fat **13g.**
Saturated fat **5g.**
Sodium **145mg.**

2¾ cups all-purpose flour
3 tsp. baking powder
¾ cup, plus 2 tbsp. sugar
⅔ cup unsalted butter
½ cup polyunsaturated margarine
4 eggs
1½ tbsp. cocoa powder

Preheat the oven to 325° F. Grease an 8-inch-diameter springform pan. Line the pan with wax paper and grease the paper.

Sift the flour and baking powder into a mixing bowl. Add the sugar, butter, margarine, and eggs. Mix them together, then beat the batter with a wooden spoon for two to three minutes, until it is smooth and glossy. Transfer half of the batter to another bowl.

Dissolve the cocoa in 3 tablespoons of boiling water and blend the paste until it is smooth. Stir the cocoa mixture into one of the bowls of batter.

Transfer alternate spoonfuls of plain and chocolate batter to the pan. Tap the pan to level the batter, and swirl a knife through it to create a marbled effect.

Bake the cake in the center of the oven until risen, lightly browned, and springy when touched in the center—50 to 55 minutes. Loosen the edges with a knife, turn the cake out onto a wire rack, and remove the lining paper. Let the cake cool completely.

EDITOR'S NOTE: *To vary the chocolate marble cake, add 1 teaspoon of grated orange zest to the plain batter. To make a coffee marble cake, replace the dissolved cocoa with 3 tablespoons of very strong black coffee.*

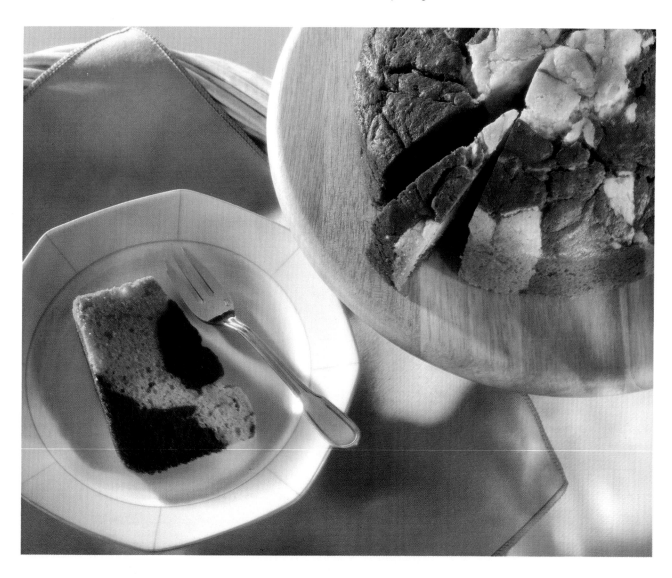

Apricot and Pine-Nut Roll

THIS CAKE IS FILLED AND ROLLED AS SOON AS IT COMES OUT OF
THE OVEN, WHILE THE SPONGE CAKE IS STILL FLEXIBLE,
SO THE FILLING MUST BE PREPARED BEFORE THE CAKE IS BAKED.

Serves 12
Working time: about 40 minutes
Total time: about 1 hour and 15 minutes

Calories **145**
Protein **5g.**
Cholesterol **35mg.**
Total fat **5g.**
Saturated fat **0g.**
Sodium **50mg.**

1⅓ cups dried apricots
1¼ cups fresh orange juice
2 tbsp. plain low-fat yogurt
2 eggs
¼ cup light brown sugar
½ cup whole wheat flour
½ tsp. baking powder
¾ cup pine nuts, finely ground
2 egg whites
1 tbsp. sugar

Preheat the oven to 350° F. Grease a 9-by-13-inch jelly-roll pan. Line the pan with wax paper and grease the paper.

Put the apricots and orange juice in a saucepan. Bring the juice to a boil and simmer the apricots for about 10 minutes, until they are tender and have absorbed nearly all the orange juice. Allow the fruit to cool for 10 minutes, then puree it with the yogurt in a blender or food processor.

Put the eggs and brown sugar in a bowl and set it over a pan of hot, but not boiling, water. Beat the mixture until it becomes thick and creamy *(page 12)*. Remove the bowl from the saucepan and continue to beat until the mixture falls in a ribbon from the spoon. Sift the flour with the baking powder into another bowl, and mix in ½ cup of the pine nuts. In a third bowl, beat the egg whites until they are stiff but not dry. Fold the flour mixture, together with one-third of the egg whites, into the beaten eggs and sugar. Then fold in the remaining egg whites.

Pour the mixture into the prepared pan and tap the pan to level the batter. Bake the cake in the center of the oven for 10 to 15 minutes until well risen, lightly browned, and springy when touched in the center. Meanwhile, place a piece of wax paper on the work surface. Mix the remaining pine nuts with the sugar, and sprinkle them evenly on the paper.

As soon as the cake comes out of the oven, turn it out onto the nuts. Working quickly, remove the lining paper from the cake and cut away the crisp edges from all four sides. Spread the apricot puree to the edge of the long sides and to within ½ inch of the short sides. With the help of the paper, roll the cake up, starting at one short side. Hold the roll for 30 seconds, until it retains its shape. Put the roll on a wire rack to cool.

EDITOR'S NOTE: *Four large oranges yield about 1¼ cups of orange juice.*

Raspberry Roll

THE CREAM CHEESE FILLING WOULD MELT IF THIS CAKE WERE FILLED AND ROLLED AS SOON AS IT CAME OUT OF THE OVEN. SO THAT THE CAKE SETS PROPERLY, IT IS ROLLED AROUND A SHEET OF PAPER WHEN HOT. WHEN THE CAKE IS COOL BUT STILL FLEXIBLE, IT IS FILLED AND ROLLED AGAIN.

Serves 12
Working time: about 40 minutes
Total time: about 1 hour and 15 minutes

Calories **110**
Protein **5g.**
Cholesterol **55mg.**
Total fat **4g.**
Saturated fat **2g.**
Sodium **50mg.**

2 eggs
¼ cup light brown sugar
¾ cup whole wheat flour
½ tsp. baking powder
⅓ cup rolled oats
2 egg whites
½ tbsp. sugar
6 oz. cream cheese
2 tbsp. plain low-fat yogurt
2 tsp. honey
1 cup fresh raspberries, or frozen raspberries, thawed
½ cup confectioners' sugar, for icing

Preheat the oven to 350° F. Grease a 9-by-13-inch jelly-roll pan. Line the bottom of the pan with wax paper and then grease the paper.

Put the eggs and brown sugar in a bowl set over a pan of hot, but not boiling, water. Beat by hand or with an electric mixer until the mixture is thick and creamy *(page 12)*. Remove the bowl from the saucepan and continue to beat until the mixture falls in a ribbon when the beater is lifted. Sift the flour with the baking powder into another bowl, and mix in the oats. In a third bowl, beat the egg whites until they are stiff but not dry. Fold the flour mixture, together with one-third of the egg whites, into the egg and sugar mixture. Then fold in the remaining egg whites.

Pour the mixture into the prepared pan and tap the pan against the work surface to level the batter. Bake the cake in the center of the oven for 10 to 15 minutes, until well risen, lightly browned, and springy when touched in the center.

Place a piece of wax paper on the work surface and sprinkle it with the sugar. Turn out the cake onto the sugar. Working quickly, detach the lining paper from the cake and trim away the crisp edges on all four sides of the cake. Cover the cake with a clean sheet of wax paper and roll up the cake with the paper inside *(below)*. Transfer the roll to a wire rack to cool.

In a bowl, mix the cream cheese with the yogurt and honey. Reserve four raspberries and gently fold the remainder into the cream cheese. As soon as the cake is cool, unroll it and remove the paper. Spread the filling evenly over the cake to within ½ inch of the short sides and right to the edge of the long sides. Roll up the cake tightly and place it on a plate.

Sift the confectioners' sugar into a small bowl and mix in 1 tablespoon of boiling water. Press one of the reserved raspberries through a nylon sieve set over the bowl, and stir the juice into the icing in order to make it a pale pink color. Beat the icing until it is smooth and glossy, and then dribble the icing over the roll. Cut the remaining raspberries in half and distribute them over the top of the cake. Serve the raspberry roll when the icing has set.

Rolling a Rectangle of Sponge Cake

1 *TRIMMING AND CUTTING. After turning the sponge cake out onto sugar-covered wax paper, trim away the crisp edges of the cake with a large knife; if left on, the edges might buckle when the cake is rolled. To initiate the rolling with ease, cut a shallow groove about 1 inch from one short end of the cake.*

2 *ROLLING THE CAKE. Working quickly, cover the sponge cake with a second piece of wax paper. Lift one end of the bottom sheet of paper so that the cake starts to roll up with the top sheet of paper inside. Handling the cake through the bottom sheet of paper, nudge it along to complete the roll.*

Angel Cake with Mango Filling

Serves 8
Working time: about 30 minutes
Total time: about 5 hours

Calories **150**
Protein **3g.**
Cholesterol **0mg.**
Total fat **1g.**
Saturated fat **0g.**
Sodium **40mg.**

5 egg whites
⅛ tsp. salt
¾ cup, plus 2 tbsp. sugar
½ lemon, finely grated zest only
1 tbsp. fresh lemon juice
2 tbsp. all-purpose flour
3 tbsp. cornstarch
confectioners' sugar to decorate
Mango filling
1 mango
⅓ cup plain low-fat yogurt
1½ tsp. unflavored powdered gelatin

Preheat the oven to 350° F. Lightly grease a 5-by-9-inch loaf pan. Line the base with wax paper, and grease the paper. Whisk the egg whites with the salt until the whites stand in stiff peaks *(page 12)*. Whisk in ½ cup of the sugar, 1 tablespoon at a time, until the mixture is thick and glossy, then beat in the lemon zest and juice. Mix the remaining sugar with the flour and cornstarch, and whisk them in 1 tablespoon at a time.

Transfer the mixture to the prepared pan and bake it for 35 to 40 minutes, until the cake is risen and firm to the touch. Let it cool in the pan.

Meanwhile, make the filling. Peel the mango and cut all the flesh away from the pit. Puree the fruit in a food processor or blender: There should be about ¾ cup of puree. Mix the puree with the yogurt. Sprinkle the gelatin over 2 tablespoons of hot water in a small bowl and place the bowl in a pan of simmering water for about 10 minutes. When the water has been absorbed, add 1 or 2 tablespoons of the puree to it. Stir the gelatin-fruit mixture into the rest of the puree.

Cut down into the cake ¾ inch away from the sides to within ¾ inch of the base. Scoop out the center with a spoon, leaving a shell with walls and a bottom about ¾-inch thick. Pour the puree into the shell and cover it with some of the cake trimmings to restore the cake to its original depth. Cover it with plastic wrap and chill it for at least two hours to allow the puree to set.

Using a knife, loosen the edges of the cake and invert it onto a serving plate. Dust the cake with the confectioners' sugar.

EDITOR'S NOTE: *The mango puree may be replaced with a puree of fresh apricots or peaches.*

Vanilla Angel Cake

ANGEL FOOD CAKE CONTAINS NO FAT AT ALL, AND IT IS SWEET
ENOUGH TO BE ENJOYED WITHOUT FROSTING OR GAR-
NISH. LEAVENED WITH MANY EGG WHITES, THE CAKE DOUBLES
IN SIZE DURING BAKING. FOR SUCCESS WITH A
LARGE ANGEL FOOD CAKE SUCH AS THIS, A TUBE CAKE PAN IS
ESSENTIAL; WITHOUT THE TUBE, THE EDGE OF THIS VOLU-
MINOUS CAKE WOULD DRY OUT BEFORE THE CENTER HAD SET.

Serves 16
Working time: about 40 minutes
Total time: about 4 hours

Calories **120**
Protein **2g.**
Cholesterol **0mg.**
Total fat **0g.**
Saturated fat **0g.**
Sodium **30mg.**

1 cup cake flour
1 cup confectioners' sugar
10 large egg whites
1 tsp. cream of tartar
½ tsp. pure vanilla extract
½ tsp. almond extract
1 cup sugar

Preheat the oven to 375° F.

Sift the flour and confectioners' sugar together into
a bowl. Put the egg whites, cream of tartar, and vanilla
and almond extracts into a large, grease-free bowl—
preferably of unlined copper, which reacts chemically
with the egg whites to strengthen the walls of the air
bubbles. Using a hand-held electric mixer or, for the
copper bowl, a large balloon whisk, beat the egg
whites until they form soft peaks. Beat in the granulated sugar 1 tablespoon at a time, and continue beating until the whites form stiff peaks. Fold in the flour
and confectioners' sugar mixture one quarter at a
time. Do not overmix: Fold only until the flour disap-
pears into the egg white.

Spoon the batter into an ungreased 10-inch tube
pan. Run a knife through the mixture to expel exces-
sively large air bubbles.

Bake the angel cake for 40 to 45 minutes, until the
mixture springs back when lightly pressed with your
fingertip. Invert the pan onto a wire rack and let the
cake stand upside down in its pan for about two hours,
until it has cooled completely.

Gently pull the cake away from the side of the pan
with a knife; it will then come out easily. Place the
angel food cake on a serving plate and remove any
loose fragments of browned cake from its surface.

Cherry-Almond Cake

Serves 16
Working time: about 25 minutes
Total time: about 1 day

Calories **220**
Protein **3g.**
Cholesterol **30g.**
Total fat **14g.**
Saturated fat **3g.**
Sodium **115mg.**

¾ cup polyunsaturated margarine
¾ cup, plus 2 tbsp. sugar
1⅔ cups all-purpose flour
1¼ tsp. baking powder
3 tbsp. cornstarch
¼ cup ground almonds
2 eggs
1 tbsp. lemon juice
½ cup sliced almonds
¾ cup candied cherries, sliced

Preheat the oven to 325° F. Line an 8-inch-square cake pan with parchment paper.

With a wooden spoon, cream the margarine and sugar together until very pale and fluffy. Sift the flour, baking powder, and cornstarch together into another bowl, then mix in the ground almonds. Beat the eggs into the creamed mixture, one at a time, following each egg with 1 tablespoon of the dry ingredients. Add the lemon juice and the remaining dry ingredients. Chop about two-thirds of the sliced almonds and stir them into the mixture, together with ½ cup of the sliced cherries.

Pour the mixture into the prepared pan and level the top. Sprinkle the remaining sliced almonds and sliced cherries over the surface of the cake and bake it for one and a quarter to one and a half hours, until firm to the touch and a light golden brown. Test the cake with a skewer; if the skewer comes out clean, the cake is done. Leave the cake in the pan for a minute or two; it will shrink away from the sides. Turn the cake out onto a wire rack to cool. With the lining paper still in place, wrap the cake in foil and let it stand for 24 hours before cutting it.

Spiced Sherry Cake

Serves 16
Working time: about 40 minutes
Total time: about 2 hours

Calories **80**
Protein **3g.**
Cholesterol **15mg.**
Total fat **8g.**
Saturated fat **2g.**
Sodium **115mg.**

1¼ cup golden raisins
4 tbsp. sherry
½ cup polyunsaturated margarine
⅔ cup light brown sugar
1 egg, beaten
1⅓ cups all-purpose flour
1 tsp. baking soda
½ tsp. ground cinnamon
½ tsp. grated nutmeg
⅛ tsp. ground cloves
⅓ cup walnuts, finely chopped
½ cup yogurt cheese (Glossary, page 140)
2 tbsp. confectioners' sugar
16 walnut halves

Preheat the oven to 350° F. Thoroughly grease two 8-inch round cake pans. Line their bases with wax paper and grease the paper.

Put the golden raisins in a saucepan with the sherry and 4 tablespoons of water, and bring the liquid to a boil. Simmer the raisins gently for about five minutes, until the liquid has been absorbed. Remove the pan from the heat and let the raisins cool, so that they will release some of the liquid.

In a mixing bowl, cream the margarine and sugar until pale and fluffy, then beat in the egg with a wooden spoon. Sift the flour, together with the baking soda, cinnamon, nutmeg, and cloves, into another bowl. Gradually fold the spiced flour, alternately with the raisins and their liquid, into the creamed margarine. Then fold in the chopped walnuts.

Divide the mixture between the prepared pans and level the surfaces. Bake the cakes for 30 to 35 minutes, until firm to the touch. Leave them in the pans for five minutes, then loosen the edges of the cakes with a knife and turn them out onto a wire rack. Take care not to damage the cakes; the high proportion of liquid makes them very fragile. Allow the cakes to cool with the lining paper still attached.

Carefully peel off the paper and stand one cake on a serving plate. Spread it with the yogurt cheese and cover it with the second layer. Dredge the top with the confectioners' sugar and, with a sharp knife, mark the cake into 16 slices. Arrange the walnut halves around the top of the cake.

Saffron Fruit Cake

MORE COMMONLY KNOWN AS A SPICE FOR SAVORY DISHES,
SAFFRON IS ALSO INCLUDED FOR ITS GOLDEN COLOR AND
DISTINCTIVE AROMA IN MANY TRADITIONAL CAKES.

Serves 24
Working time: about 25 minutes
Total time: about 4 hours and 30 minutes

Calories **192**	
Protein **3g.**	2 tsp. saffron strands
Cholesterol **25mg.**	4 cups whole wheat flour
Total fat **8g.**	4 tsp. baking powder
Saturated fat **1g.**	¾ cup polyunsaturated margarine
Sodium **75mg.**	⅔ cup light brown sugar
	1 cup dried apricots, 4 reserved, the rest chopped
	7 dried figs, 3 reserved, the rest chopped
	2 eggs
	½ cup confectioners' sugar, sifted

Preheat the oven to 325° F. Grease an 8-inch-square cake pan. Line it with wax paper and grease the paper.

Put the saffron strands in a small saucepan with ¾ cup of water and bring the water to a boil. Remove the pan from the heat and let the saffron liquid cool.

Sift the flour and baking powder together into a mixing bowl and, using your fingertips or the back of a wooden spoon, rub in the margarine until the mix-ture resembles bread crumbs. Stir in the light brown sugar, chopped apricots, chopped figs, eggs, and all but 2 tablespoons of the saffron strands and liquid. Beat the mixture with a wooden spoon for one minute.

Spoon the mixture into the prepared pan and level the top with a small spatula. Bake the cake in the center of the oven until risen, golden brown, and springy in the center—55 to 60 minutes. Leave the cake in the pan to cool for five minutes, then turn it out and remove the lining paper. Invert the cake onto a wire rack and leave it until completely cool.

Halve the reserved apricots and slice the reserved figs. Arrange them on top of the cake. Mix the con-fectioners' sugar thoroughly with the remaining saf-fron liquid. Dribble the icing over the cake. Let it set.

EDITOR'S NOTE: *The apricots and figs can be replaced by other dried fruits, such as prunes, pears, and peaches.*

Saffron-Currant Loaf

Serves 20
Working time: about 40 minutes
Total time: about 14 hours

Calories **160**
Protein **3g.**
Cholesterol **10mg.**
Total fat **4g.**
Saturated fat **2g.**
Sodium **10mg.**

¼ tsp. saffron strands
4 cups bread flour
⅛ tsp. salt
6 tbsp. unsalted butter
2 tbsp. light brown sugar
1 lemon, grated zest only
1¼ cups currants
¼ cup mixed candied peel, chopped
1 cake (.6 oz.) fresh yeast, or 1 envelope (¼ oz.) active dry yeast plus 1 tsp. sugar
⅔ cup scalded, tepid skim milk
1 tbsp. honey

Infuse the saffron in ⅔ cup of boiling water overnight, then strain the liquid.

Grease an 8-inch round cake pan.

Sift the flour and salt into a bowl and, using your fingertips or the back of a wooden spoon, rub in the butter until the mixture resembles fine bread crumbs. Stir in the sugar, lemon zest, currants, and candied peel. Blend the fresh yeast or the dry yeast and sugar with the milk. If you use dry yeast, leave the mixture in a warm place for about 15 minutes, until frothy.

Warm the saffron liquid in a small saucepan and mix it, together with the yeast mixture, into the dry ingredients. Turn the dough out onto a floured surface and knead it for about five minutes. Shape the dough to fit the pan. Put the dough in the pan and cover it with oiled plastic wrap. Leave the dough in a warm place for one to one and a half hours, until it has doubled in size and springs back when lightly pressed with a floured fingertip. Meanwhile, preheat the oven to 400° F.

Remove the plastic wrap and bake the loaf for 30 minutes. Reduce the temperature to 350° F. and bake it for 25 to 30 minutes more, until it is well risen, browned, and firm to the touch. Turn the loaf out onto a wire rack. While the loaf is still warm, brush its top all over with a wet pastry brush dipped in the honey. Let the loaf cool.

Poppy-Seed Twist

Serves 12
Working time: about 1 hour
Total time: about 4 hours

Calories **240**
Protein **6g.**
Cholesterol **30mg.**
Total fat **10g.**
Saturated fat **4g.**
Sodium **80mg.**

1 cake (.6 oz.) fresh yeast, or 1 envelope (¼ oz.) active dry yeast
6 tbsp. scalded, tepid milk
2 cups bread flour
⅛ tsp. salt
2 tbsp. unsalted butter, melted
2 tbsp. sugar
1 egg, beaten
½ lemon, finely grated zest only
3 tbsp. confectioners' sugar
1 tbsp. fresh lemon juice

Poppy-seed and raisin filling
⅔ cup poppy seeds
⅔ cup raisins, chopped
1 cup milk
2 tbsp. cornstarch
1 egg yolk
2 tbsp. unsalted butter
½ cup hazelnuts, toasted and chopped

Mix the fresh yeast with the milk and about 1 table-spoon of the flour in a bowl, or reconstitute the active dry yeast according to the manufacturer's instructions, adding the milk and 1 tablespoon of the flour. Leave the mixture in a warm place until it froths—about 10 to 15 minutes.

Sift the remaining flour into a bowl with the salt. Add the butter, sugar, egg, lemon zest, and yeast mixture, and work the combination into a soft dough. Knead the dough on a lightly floured surface for five minutes. Put the dough in an oiled bowl, cover it with oiled plastic wrap, and leave it in a warm place to rise until doubled in volume—one to two hours.

Meanwhile, preheat the oven to 400° F., grease a 9-inch springform pan, and make the filling. Put the poppy seeds and raisins in a saucepan with half the milk and simmer gently for five to seven minutes, until the poppy seeds have swelled and most of the milk has been absorbed. Mix the cornstarch and egg yolk with the remaining milk, and add the mixture to the pan.

Cook, stirring, until the mixture thickens. Remove the pan from the heat and stir in the butter. Allow the filling to cool, then stir in the hazelnuts.

To make the twist, roll out the dough on a lightly floured surface, forming a rectangle about 15 by 18 inches. Spread it with the poppy-seed and raisin filling. Roll up the dough into a cylinder, cut it in half lengthwise, and twist the two halves together *(below)*.

Place the dough in the prepared pan and join the ends of the braid to make a circle. Bake the poppy-seed twist for about 35 minutes, until golden brown. Transfer it to a wire rack. Mix the confectioners' sugar and lemon juice together and brush them over the cake. Let the poppy-seed twist cool a little; it is best served slightly warm.

EDITOR'S NOTE: *To toast hazelnuts, place them on a baking sheet in a preheated 350° F. oven for 10 minutes.*

Twisting the Dough

1 ROLLING AND SLICING. *Spread the poppy-seed filling evenly over the dough, leaving about 1 inch of dough uncovered around the edge. Roll up the dough from one side, enclosing the filling.*

2 DIVIDING THE ROLL. *With a sharp knife, trim the ends of the dough to make a neat cylinder, then slice the cylinder down the middle, cutting it in half lengthwise.*

3 TWISTING THE DOUGH. *With the cut sides facing up, lay one length of poppy-seed dough across the middle of the other. Twist the two lengths over each other, working outward from the center in one direction, then in the other.*

4 LAYING THE CAKE IN THE PAN. *Keeping the filling side up, lift the dough carefully into the pan. Press the ends together, forming a circle.*

Caraway Sponge Cake

Serves 12
Working time: about 25 minutes
Total time: about 3 hours and 30 minutes

Calories **125**
Protein **3g.**
Cholesterol **60mg.**
Total fat **3g.**
Saturated fat **0g.**
Sodium **70mg.**

3 eggs, separated
⅔ cup light brown sugar
1 cup all-purpose flour
1 tsp. baking powder
1½ tbsp. cornstarch
2 tsp. polyunsaturated margarine
1 tbsp. orange-flower water
1 tsp. caraway seeds
confectioners' sugar to decorate

Preheat the oven to 400° F. Grease a round cake pan 8 inches in diameter or a petal cake pan about 7 inches in diameter. Line the pan with parchment paper.

Whisk the egg whites until they stand in firm peaks *(page 12)*. Gradually whisk in the sugar, 1 tablespoon at a time, then quickly fold in the egg yolks. Sift the flour, baking powder, and cornstarch together two or three times into another bowl to aerate them thoroughly. Heat the margarine in a small saucepan until the margarine melts; remove the pan from the heat, and add the orange-flower water and 2 tablespoons of water. Using a mixing spoon or a rubber spatula, fold the flour mixture quickly and evenly through the cake mixture, followed by the melted mixture and the caraway seeds. Pour the batter into the prepared pan, and bake the sponge cake until well risen, golden brown, and firm to the touch. Cooking time will be 25 to 30 minutes in the round pan, 30 to 40 minutes in the petal pan.

Turn the cake out onto a wire rack and let it cool, then remove the paper. Before serving the cake, sift confectioners' sugar lightly over the top.

Ginger Kugelhopf

A SPECIALITY OF GERMANY, AUSTRIA, AND ALSACE, THE
KUGELHOPF IS A YEAST CAKE BAKED IN A FLUTED RING MOLD.

Serves 12
Working time: about 40 minutes
Total time: about 4 hours

Calories **167**
Protein **4g.**
Cholesterol **80mg.**
Total fat **7g.**
Saturated fat **3g.**
Sodium **115mg.**

1 cake (.6 oz.) fresh yeast, or
1 envelope (¼ oz.) active dry yeast
2 tbsp. sugar
2 cups bread flour
½ tsp. salt
1 tsp. ground cinnamon
½ tsp. ground ginger
4 tbsp. unsalted butter, melted
3 eggs, beaten
2 tbsp. ginger preserved in syrup, finely chopped
¼ cup dried apricots, finely chopped
1 oz. semisweet chocolate
2 tsp. pine nuts

In a small bowl, mix the yeast and sugar with 4 tablespoons of tepid water and 1 tablespoon of the flour. Set the mixture in a warm place for 10 to 15 minutes, until it is frothy.

Mix the remaining flour, the salt, and the spices in a bowl. Add the butter, eggs, ginger, apricots, and yeast mixture, and beat the batter with a wooden spoon until the ingredients have combined evenly. Cover the batter with oiled plastic wrap and leave it in a warm place for one to two hours, until it has doubled in volume.

Generously butter an 8-inch kugelhopf mold or Bundt pan. Stir the risen batter quickly, then spoon it into the prepared mold. Cover it with oiled plastic wrap and let it rise again until it almost reaches the top of the mold—45 minutes to 1 hour. Meanwhile, preheat the oven to 400° F.

Remove the plastic wrap and bake the kugelhopf for about 30 minutes, until golden brown and firm to the touch. Leave it in the mold for 30 minutes, then turn it out onto a wire rack. When the cake has cooled completely, melt the chocolate in a bowl over a saucepan of hot, but not boiling, water and dribble it onto the cake from a spoon or a wax paper pastry bag *(page 17)*. Sprinkle the cake with pine nuts. Serve it when the chocolate has set.

Steamed Malt Loaf

COOKED BY STEAMING INSTEAD OF BAKING, THIS LOAF
ACQUIRES A MOIST, RESILIENT TEXTURE. IT IS BEST AFTER TWO
OR THREE DAYS, WHEN ITS FLAVOR HAS FULLY DEVELOPED.

Serves 12
Working time: about 15 minutes
Total time: about 4 hours

Calories **205**
Protein **4g.**
Cholesterol **0mg.**
Total fat **1g.**
Saturated fat **0g.**
Sodium **60mg.**

½ cup barley malt
1¼ cups whole wheat flour
1¼ cups rye flour
1¼ cups cornmeal
1½ tsp. baking powder
3 tbsp. buttermilk
1 cup raisins
¼ cup molasses

Grease and flour a 4-by-10-inch loaf pan. To make the
cake, reserve 2 tablespoons of the barley malt for
glazing, and stir the remaining barley malt well with all
the other ingredients. Transfer the batter into the prepared pan and level the surface. Cover the pan loosely
with greased foil, and set it on a trivet in a fish poacher
or large flameproof casserole. Pour boiling water into
the fish poacher or casserole until it comes halfway up
the sides of the loaf pan. Put a lid on the poacher, set
it on the stove, and adjust the heat so that the water
simmers. Cook the loaf for about two hours, until it is
risen and firm to the touch. Leave the loaf in the pan
for 10 minutes.

Turn the malt loaf onto a wire rack. Brush the loaf
with the reserved malt while it is still warm, then allow
the loaf to cool.

Vinegar Cake

THE VINEGAR REACTS WITH THE BAKING SODA TO RELEASE CARBON DIOXIDE, WHICH LEAVENS THE CAKE. THIS PROCESS DOES NOT AFFECT THE FLAVOR.

Serves 20
Working time: about 20 minutes
Total time: about 3 hours and 30 minutes

Calories **220**
Protein **2g.**
Cholesterol **0mg.**
Total fat **8g.**
Saturated fat **2g.**
Sodium **130mg.**

2¾ cups all-purpose flour
1 cup rice flour
½ tsp. ground allspice
1⅓ cups polyunsaturated margarine
1 cup raisins
¾ cup golden raisins
¾ cup candied citrus peel
¾ cup milk
3 tbsp. cider vinegar
1 tsp. baking soda
⅔ cup confectioners' sugar
1½ tbsp. fresh lemon juice

Preheat the oven to 325° F. Grease a deep 5-by-9-inch loaf pan. Line it with wax paper and grease the paper.

Put the flour, rice flour, and allspice into a mixing bowl. Add the margarine and rub it in with your fingertips or the back of a wooden spoon until the mixture resembles bread crumbs. Stir in both kinds of raisins and the candied peel.

Heat the milk in a saucepan until it is tepid. Stir in the vinegar and baking soda, which will froth up. Immediately add this liquid to the fruit mixture in the bowl, so as not to lose too much of the gas. Stir with a wooden spoon to blend the ingredients, then beat the mixture to achieve a smooth, soft consistency. Spoon the mixture into the prepared pan, and level the top with a small spatula.

Bake the cake in the center of the oven until well risen, golden brown, and springy when touched in the middle—about an hour and 10 minutes. Loosen the edges with a knife, turn the cake out of the pan onto a wire rack, and remove the lining paper. Let the cake cool completely.

With a wooden spoon, beat the confectioners' sugar with the lemon juice in a small bowl until smooth. Spoon the icing into a wax-paper pastry bag *(page 17)*, and pipe a lattice design over the top of the cake. Let the cake stand until the icing has set.

Apricot and Orange Loaf

THE SOY FLOUR USED IN THIS RECIPE IS HIGH IN PROTEIN: ONE
SLICE OF THE CAKE PROVIDES 10 PERCENT OF AN ADULT'S DAILY
PROTEIN REQUIREMENT.

Serves 16
Working time: about 30 minutes
Total time: about 4 hours and 30 minutes

Calories **175**
Protein **7g.**
Cholesterol **40mg.**
Total fat **7g.**
Saturated fat **3g.**
Sodium **65mg.**

1 cup dried apricots, chopped
1¼ cups golden raisins
⅔ cup fresh orange juice
1 tsp. finely grated orange zest
4 tbsp. unsalted butter
2 cups soy flour
2 tsp. baking powder
½ cup walnuts, chopped
¼ cup light brown sugar
2 eggs, beaten
Apricot-walnut topping
1 tbsp. honey
2 tbsp. fresh orange juice
¼ cup walnuts, chopped
6 dried apricots, chopped

Preheat the oven to 325° F. Grease a 4½-by-8-inch
loaf pan. Line the bottom and two long sides with wax
paper, and grease the paper.

Put the apricots, golden raisins, orange juice, zest,
and butter in a saucepan. Heat gently, stirring occasionally, until the butter has melted; remove the saucepan from the heat. Sift the soy flour and baking powder into a bowl. Mix in the walnuts and sugar. With a
wooden spoon, stir in the eggs and the fruit mixture,
then beat the batter until it is smooth and glossy.

Spoon the mixture into the prepared pan and level
the top with a small spatula. Bake the loaf in the center
of the oven until risen, lightly browned, and springy
when touched in the middle—about one and a quarter
hours. Loosen the edges with a small spatula, turn the
loaf out of the pan onto a wire rack, and remove the
lining paper. Let the loaf cool to room temperature.

To make the topping, warm the honey and orange
juice in a small saucepan. Boil for 30 seconds, stirring
occasionally. Put the walnuts in a small bowl and stir
in half of the honey mixture. Add the apricots to the
liquid remaining in the pan and heat gently for one
minute. Arrange the walnuts in a row down the center
of the cake and spread the apricots on either side. Let
the loaf stand for a few minutes to allow the topping
to cool and set.

Raisin Tea Loaf

Serves 20
Working time: about 20 minutes
Total time: about 4 hours and 30 minutes

Calories **180**
Protein **4g.**
Cholesterol **20mg.**
Total fat **0g.**
Saturated fat **0g.**
Sodium **90mg.**

1¼ cups currants
1¼ cups golden raisins
1¼ cups raisins
⅔ cup light brown sugar
1¼ cups warm tea, strained
3 tbsp. low-sugar marmalade
4 cups whole wheat flour
4 tsp. baking powder
1 egg

Preheat the oven to 325° F. Grease two 4-by-8-inch loaf pans. Line the bottoms and long sides with wax paper, and grease the paper.

Put the currants, golden raisins, raisins, and sugar in a mixing bowl with the tea and 2 tablespoons of the marmalade. Stir well, cover the bowl with plastic wrap, and let the fruit stand for about 30 minutes, until it plumps up.

When the tea has cooled, sift the flour and baking powder into the fruit mixture, adding the bran left in the sieve. Add the egg, and mix the batter well with a wooden spoon.

Divide the mixture equally between the two prepared pans; level the tops with a spatula. Bake the loaves in the center of the oven until risen, lightly browned, and springy when touched in the middle— about one and a quarter hours. Loosen the edges with a knife, turn the loaves onto a wire rack, and remove the lining paper. Let the loaves cool completely.

Heat the remaining marmalade in a small saucepan with 1 teaspoon of water. Boil the mixture for 30 seconds. Brush the tops of both loaves with marmalade, and slice them only when it has set.

EDITOR'S NOTE: *Wrapped separately in plastic wrap or foil, the loaves will keep well for two weeks in a cool place.*

Spiced Apricot Rehrücken Cake

THIS CAKE IS NAMED AFTER A RIDGED LOAF PAN CALLED
REHRÜCKEN BECAUSE IT LOOKS LIKE A SADDLE OF VENISON.

Serves 10
Working time: about 35 minutes
Total time: about 4 hours

Calories **225**
Protein **4g.**
Cholesterol **45mg.**
Total fat **7g.**
Saturated fat **4g.**
Sodium **80mg.**

1⅔ cups all-purpose flour
1½ tsp. baking powder
½ tsp. grated nutmeg
4 tbsp. polyunsaturated margarine
⅓ cup light brown sugar
1 orange, grated zest only
⅔ cup dried apricots, finely chopped
1 egg
1 tbsp. molasses
4½ tbsp. skim milk
Nutmeg buttercream
2 tbsp. unsalted butter
½ cup confectioners' sugar
⅛ tsp. grated nutmeg
½ tsp. fresh orange juice
7 dried apricots, halved

Preheat the oven to 350° F. Thoroughly grease a 10-inch rehrücken loaf pan or a 5-by-9-inch loaf pan.

Sift the flour and baking powder into a bowl, and mix in the nutmeg. Add the margarine, rubbing it with your fingertips or the back of a wooden spoon until the mixture resembles fine bread crumbs. Stir in the sugar, orange zest, and chopped apricots. In another bowl, beat together the egg, molasses, and skim milk; add them to the first bowl and blend the ingredients thoroughly with a wooden spoon.

Turn the mixture into the prepared pan and level the top. Bake the cake for about 50 minutes, until it has risen to the top of the pan; it should be firm to the touch and just beginning to shrink from the sides of the pan. Turn the cake out onto a wire rack and let it cool completely.

Meanwhile, cream the butter until it is soft. Sift in the confectioners' sugar, and then add the nutmeg. Beat the mixture with a wooden spoon. Add a few drops of orange juice to give a piping consistency. Spoon the buttercream into a pastry bag fitted with a medium-size star tip, and pipe a continuous row of shells along the top of the cake. Alternatively, spoon the buttercream down the length of the cake. Decorate the cake with the apricot halves.

Fig Cake Encased in Shortcrust

Serves 10
Working time: about 45 minutes
Total time: about 3 hours and 30 minutes

Calories **230**
Protein **5g.**
Cholesterol **50mg.**
Total fat **11g.**
Saturated fat **5g.**
Sodium **120mg.**

¾ cup dried figs, chopped
1 cup dried pears, chopped
⅓ cup dried dates, chopped
2 tbsp. unsalted butter, cut into small pieces
2 tbsp. brandy
½ cup walnuts, chopped
1 egg, beaten
¼ cup all-purpose flour
½ tsp. ground cinnamon
¼ tsp. ground cloves
⅛ tsp. salt
confectioners' sugar to decorate
Pastry crust
1 cup all-purpose flour
4 tbsp. unsalted butter
beaten egg white to glaze

Put the figs, pears, and dates into a saucepan with 6 tablespoons of water. Simmer gently until the fruit is soft and the water has been absorbed—seven to eight minutes. Add the butter and stir until it has melted. Let the mixture cool, then beat in the brandy, walnuts, egg, flour, cinnamon, cloves, and salt.

Preheat the oven to 350° F.

To make the pastry, sift the flour into a bowl. Rub in the butter with your fingertips or the back of a wooden spoon, and mix in about 4 teaspoons of ice water; add only enough water to make a firm dough. Roll out two-thirds of the pastry on a lightly floured surface, forming a rectangle large enough to cover the base and sides of a 4-by-8-inch loaf pan. Transfer the pastry to the pan and press against the base and sides so that it covers the pan with an even thickness.

Spoon the filling into the pan and level the surface. Trim the pastry until it is level with the top of the pan, then fold the pastry walls in over the filling. Add the trimmings to the reserved pastry and roll it out into a rectangle that fits the top of the cake exactly. Trim the edges of the pastry lid. Brush the pastry with beaten egg white and lay the pastry, brushed side down, on top of the cake. Press the edge of the lid firmly so that it sticks to the folded pastry walls. Using a fork, mark a crisscross pattern and a decorative border on the pastry lid. Brush the lid with beaten egg white.

Bake the cake for 40 to 45 minutes, until the pastry is pale golden. Let the cake stand in the pan for 10 minutes, then transfer it to a wire rack and allow it to cool. Dust with confectioners' sugar before serving.

Tropical Fruit Cake

Serves 24
Working time: about 30 minutes
Total time: about 5 hours

Calories **275**
Protein **4g.**
Cholesterol **45mg.**
Total fat **10g.**
Saturated fat **3g.**
Sodium **145mg.**

1 cup polyunsaturated margarine
1 cup, plus 2 tbsp. light brown sugar
4 eggs
2¾ cups all-purpose flour
3 tsp. baking powder
⅓ cup angelica or other green candied fruit, chopped
¾ cup dried papaya, chopped
¾ cup dried pineapple, chopped
¾ cup shredded coconut
½ cup banana chips, crushed
2 tbsp. skim milk
1 tbsp. apricot jam without added sugar

Preheat the oven to 350° F. Grease a 9-inch round cake pan. Line it with parchment paper.

Put the margarine, sugar, and eggs in a mixing bowl. Sift in the flour and baking powder. Reserve 2 table-spoons each of the angelica, dried papaya, dried pine-apple, and shredded coconut for decoration. Coarsely chop the rest of the shredded coconut. Add the re-maining angelica, papaya, pineapple, and coconut, as well as the banana chips and skim milk, to the bowl. Mix until the ingredients are thoroughly blended, then beat the batter firmly with a wooden spoon for two minutes, until it is smooth. Transfer the batter into the prepared pan and level the top. Bake the fruit cake for about two hours, until it is well browned and firm to the touch; a skewer inserted in the center should come out clean.

Cool the cake for five minutes in the pan, then turn it out onto a wire rack and leave it to cool completely. Peel off the lining paper. Warm the jam in a small saucepan, and brush it over the top of the cake. Sprin-kle the top of the cake with the reserved tropical fruits.

Farmhouse Fruit Cake

THE OVERNIGHT SOAKING OF THE INGREDIENTS IN TEA MAKES
THIS CAKE VERY MOIST.

Serves 10
Working time: about 20 minutes
Total time: about 1½ days

Calories **210**
Protein **2g.**
Cholesterol **0mg.**
Total fat **7g.**
Saturated fat **2g.**
Sodium **170mg.**

2 cups all-purpose flour
½ tsp. ground allspice
6 tbsp. polyunsaturated margarine
⅓ cup light brown sugar
1 cup golden raisins
⅓ cup currants
½ lemon, grated zest only
1 tsp. baking soda
2 tbsp. lemon juice
1 cup cold tea
1 tsp. sugar

Grease a 6½- to 7-inch round cake pan and line it with parchment paper.

Sift the flour and the allspice together in a bowl. Add the margarine and, using your fingertips or the back of a wooden spoon, rub it in until the mixture resembles fine bread crumbs. Stir in the brown sugar, golden raisins, currants, and lemon zest until they are evenly distributed. Whisk the baking soda into the lemon juice and add this mixture, together with the cold tea, to the dry ingredients. When the ingredients are thoroughly combined, pour the mixture into the prepared pan, level the top, and allow the mixture to stand overnight.

The following day, preheat the oven to 325° F.

Sprinkle the cake mixture with the sugar and cook it for about one and a half hours, until a skewer inserted in its center comes out clean. Turn the cake out onto a wire rack and leave it to cool. With the lining paper still in place, wrap the cake in foil and store it for 24 hours; it crumbles if sliced sooner.

Stollen

STOLLEN, THE GERMAN YEAST-LEAVENED CHRISTMAS CAKE,
IS USUALLY RICH IN BUTTER AND SOMETIMES INCLUDES
GROUND ALMONDS; THIS VERSION, WITH LESS BUTTER AND NO
ALMONDS, IS LIGHTER BUT STILL DELICIOUSLY FLAVORED
WITH DRIED FRUITS AND RUM. UNLIKE MOST YEAST CAKES,
STOLLEN SHOULD BE MADE WITH ALL-PURPOSE FLOUR RATHER
THAN BREAD FLOUR, TO GIVE IT A SOFT, CRUMBLY TEXTURE.

Serves 24
Working time: about 40 minutes
Total time: about 7 hours

Calories **135**
Protein **3g.**
Cholesterol **20mg.**
Total fat **4g.**
Saturated fat **2g.**
Sodium **15mg.**

2 cakes (1.2 oz.) fresh yeast, or 2 envelopes (½ oz.) active dry yeast
⅓ cup vanilla sugar
6 tbsp. skim milk
2 tbsp. dark rum
3¼ cups all-purpose flour
7 tbsp. unsalted butter
1 egg, beaten
⅓ cup raisins
½ cup currants
⅓ cup mixed candied peel, chopped
2 tbsp. candied cherries, chopped
2 tbsp. angelica or other green candied fruit, chopped
2 tbsp. confectioners' sugar

In a small bowl, blend the yeast with 2 tablespoons of warm water. If using dry yeast, add 1 teaspoon of the sugar to the yeast and water, and set it aside to blend in a warm place for about 20 minutes, until it froths; fresh yeast can be used immediately.

Warm the skim milk in a saucepan. Remove the pan from the heat and dissolve the sugar in the milk; add the rum and the yeast liquid. Sift the flour into a large bowl and make a well in the center. Cut 6 tablespoons of the butter into bean-size pieces and add them to the flour. Add the yeast mixture and the egg, raisins, currants, mixed peel, cherries, and angelica. Mix the ingredients with a wooden spoon and knead the dough for 10 minutes by hand on a lightly floured surface, or for four to five minutes in a large electric mixer fitted with a dough hook. Flour the bowl and return the dough to it. Cover the dough with oiled plastic wrap and let it rise in a warm place until it has doubled in size—about two hours. (It takes a long time because of all the fruit.)

Punch down the dough and knead it for two to three minutes, until smooth. On a lightly floured surface, roll the dough out into a rectangle approximately 8 by 12 inches. Fold one long side over just beyond the center, then fold the other long side to overlap the first. Press down lightly to secure the flap in position, and transfer the cake to a well-greased baking sheet. Melt the remaining butter and brush it over the surface of the stollen. Put the cake in a warm place for 20 to 30 minutes, until it has almost doubled in size. Meanwhile, preheat the oven to 375° F.

Cook the stollen for about 40 minutes, until it is well risen and browned, and the loaf sounds hollow when tapped on its base. Transfer the stollen to a wire rack and let it cool completely. Dredge the cake with the confectioners' sugar before serving.

EDITOR'S NOTE: *The stollen will freeze well for up to two months. Do not add the confectioners' sugar until the cake has thawed.*

Dundee Cake

WITH ITS VERY HIGH PROPORTION OF FRUIT, THIS MOIST, DARK CAKE IS FULL OF FLAVOR YET LIGHT IN TEXTURE.

Serves 28
Working time: about 20 minutes
Total time: about 7 hours

Calories **215**
Protein **3g.**
Cholesterol **40mg.**
Total fat **8g.**
Saturated fat **2g.**
Sodium **95mg.**

1½ cups currants
1½ cups golden raisins
1½ cups raisins
½ cup mixed candied peel, chopped
½ cup candied cherries, quartered
1 orange, grated zest and juice
2 cups whole wheat flour
1 tsp. baking powder
1 cup rolled oats
2 tsp. ground cinnamon
⅔ cup light brown sugar
2 tbsp. molasses
¾ cup polyunsaturated margarine
4 eggs, beaten
⅓ cup blanched almonds

Preheat the oven to 275° F. Grease a deep 8-inch-square cake pan and line it with two sheets of wax paper. Grease the paper. To prevent the sides and base of the cake from scorching during the long cooking, tie a double thickness of brown paper around the outside of the pan and put the pan on a baking sheet double-lined with brown paper.

Stir the currants, both kinds of raisins, the mixed peel, candied cherries, orange zest, and juice together in a small mixing bowl. Sift the flour and baking powder together into another bowl, adding the bran left in the sieve. Mix in the rolled oats, cinnamon, sugar, molasses, margarine, and eggs. Beat the mixture with a wooden spoon for two to three minutes, until it is smooth and glossy.

Stir the fruit into the cake batter. Spoon the batter into the cake pan and level the top with a small spatula. Arrange the almonds in rows on the cake.

Bake the cake in the center of the oven until risen and dark brown—two and a half to three hours. Test the cake by inserting a warm skewer or a toothpick into the center of the cake. If it is clean when removed, the cake is cooked; otherwise, return the cake to the oven and test it at 15-minute intervals.

Allow the cake to cool in the pan, then turn it out and remove the lining paper.

EDITOR'S NOTE: *Because the fruit retains moisture, this cake will keep for up to one month if it is sealed in plastic wrap or foil and stored in a cold, dry place.*

Coffee Walnut Cake

Serves 14
Working time: about 20 minutes
Total time: about 2 hours and 30 minutes

Calories **210**
Protein **4g.**
Cholesterol **30mg.**
Total fat **13g.**
Saturated fat **2g.**
Sodium **185g.**

½ cup polyunsaturated margarine
¼ cup light brown sugar
4 tbsp. honey
2 eggs, beaten
2 tbsp. strong black coffee, cooled
2 cups whole wheat flour
3 tsp. baking powder
¾ cup walnuts, coarsely chopped
10 walnut halves

Preheat the oven to 325° F.

Grease a deep 8-inch round cake pan. Line it with wax paper and grease the paper.

Put the margarine, sugar, and honey in a mixing bowl. Beat them together with a wooden spoon until light and fluffy. Add the eggs a little at a time, beating well after each addition. Beat in the coffee.

Sift in the flour and baking powder, adding the bran left in the sieve. Using a spatula or large spoon, fold the flour into the batter. Mix in the chopped walnuts. Spoon the mixture into the prepared pan. Level the top with a small spatula and arrange the walnut halves around the edge.

Bake the cake in the center of the oven until risen, lightly browned, and springy when touched in the center—50 to 55 minutes. Loosen the edges of the cake with a knife, turn it out onto a wire rack, and remove the lining paper. Let the cake cool.

Clove and Apple Loaf

Serves 20
Working time: about 20 minutes
Total time: about 4 hours

Calories **150**
Protein **4g.**
Total fat **5g.**
Saturated fat **0g.**
Cholesterol **20mg.**
Sodium **80mg.**

2 apples, cored and chopped
½ cup pecans, chopped
½ cup hazelnuts, chopped
2 tbsp. honey
1 tbsp. safflower oil
⅔ cup light brown sugar
⅔ cup cider
1 egg, beaten
2 cups whole wheat flour
1 cup rye flour
4 tsp. baking powder
1 tsp. ground cloves

Preheat the oven to 325° F. Grease a 4-by-12-inch loaf pan. Line it with wax paper and grease the paper.

Put the apples, pecans, hazelnuts, honey, oil, sugar, cider, and egg in a mixing bowl. Mix them well with a wooden spoon. Sift in the whole wheat flour with the rye flour, baking powder, and cloves, adding the bran left in the sieve. Stir until the batter is well blended, then beat for one minute until it is glossy. Spoon the batter into the prepared pan and level the top with a small spatula.

Bake the loaf in the center of the oven until risen, lightly browned, and springy when touched in the center—about one hour and 20 minutes. Loosen the edges with a knife and turn the loaf out of the pan onto a wire rack. Remove the lining paper and let the loaf cool completely.

Raisin and Ginger Buttermilk Cake

BUTTERMILK IS A LOW-FAT DAIRY FOOD, TRADITIONALLY PRODUCED AS A BY-PRODUCT OF BUTTER-MAKING BUT NOWADAYS OFTEN PREPARED BY THICKENING SKIM MILK WITH A BACTERIAL CULTURE. THIS FRUIT CAKE IS LEAVENED BY THE CARBON DIOXIDE GAS PRODUCED WHEN THE BAKING SODA ENCOUNTERS THE ACID IN THE BUTTERMILK.

Serves 16
Working time: about 20 minutes
Total time: about 5 hours

Calories **220**
Protein **3g.**
Cholesterol **0mg.**
Total fat **8g.**
Saturated fat **2g.**
Sodium **130mg.**

1⅓ cups all-purpose flour
1⅓ cups whole wheat flour
½ tsp. ground cinnamon
¼ tsp. ground ginger
⅛ tsp. grated nutmeg
⅔ cup polyunsaturated margarine
⅔ cup light brown sugar
1 lemon, grated zest only
⅔ cup currants
⅔ cup raisins
⅓ cup mixed candied peel, chopped
1 cup buttermilk
1 tbsp. molasses
¾ tsp. baking soda

Preheat the oven to 325° F. Line a 5-by-9-inch loaf pan with parchment paper.

Sift the all-purpose flour into a bowl and mix in the whole wheat flour, cinnamon, ginger, and nutmeg. Add the margarine and, using your fingertips or the back of a wooden spoon, rub it in until the mixture resembles fine bread crumbs. Mix in the sugar, lemon zest, currants, raisins, and peel. Heat the buttermilk gently in a saucepan, then stir in the molasses until it melts. Add the baking soda and stir until it froths. Combine this liquid with the dry ingredients, and mix until they are evenly blended.

Transfer the mixture to the prepared pan and level the top. Bake the buttermilk cake for about one and a quarter hours, until it is well risen and firm to the touch; a skewer inserted in the center should come out clean. Turn the cake out onto a wire rack and let it cool completely before removing the lining paper.

Banana Tofu Cake

TOFU IS A PROTEIN-RICH EXTRACT OF SOY BEANS.
IT HAS A MILD TASTE AND A TEXTURE SIMILAR
TO THAT OF RICOTTA CHEESE. AGAR, A SEAWEED PRODUCT,
IS USED BY VEGETARIANS IN PLACE OF GELATIN.

Serves 10
Working time: about 30 minutes
Total time: about 3 hours

Calories **290**
Protein **20g.**
Cholesterol **20mg.**
Total fat **10g.**
Saturated fat **4g.**
Sodium **35mg.**

1 cup pitted fresh dates, chopped, or ¾ cup dried, pitted chopped dates
1¼ cups fresh orange juice
2 large peeled bananas, sliced
1 lb. tofu
1 tbsp. agar powder
1 tsp. finely grated lemon zest
½ tsp. pumpkin pie spice
1 tbsp. apricot jam without added sugar
1 tbsp. finely chopped, skinned toasted hazelnuts

Spicy oat base

1 cup whole wheat flour
1½ cups rolled oats
⅓ cup unsalted butter, melted
3 tbsp. barley malt or honey
1 tsp. pumpkin pie spice

Preheat the oven to 350° F. To make the spicy oat base, combine the flour, oats, butter, barley malt or honey, and pumpkin pie spice in a bowl. Press them into the bottom of an 8-inch springform pan. Bake the mixture for 15 minutes, then let it cool.

Simmer the dates in the orange juice for about 12 minutes, until they are very soft. Put the dates and juice in a food processor or blender with the bananas, tofu, agar powder, lemon zest, and spice. Blend to a puree. Spoon it over the oat base and level the surface. Bake the cake for 40 to 45 minutes, until it is firm when pressed in the center with your fingertip. Allow the cake to cool in the pan.

While the cake is cooling, heat the apricot jam in a small saucepan. Press the jam through a sieve into a bowl and brush it over the surface of the cake. Sprinkle the chopped hazelnuts around the edge of the cake.

EDITOR'S NOTE: *To toast and skin hazelnuts, place them on a cookie sheet in a preheated 350° F. oven for 10 minutes. Wrap them in a towel and loosen the skins by rubbing briskly.*

Pear and Orange Upside-Down Cake

Serves 10
Working time: about 20 minutes
Total time: about 2 hours and 30 minutes

Calories **160**
Protein **2g.**
Cholesterol **0mg.**
Total fat **5g.**
Saturated fat **0g.**
Sodium **110mg.**

2 pears, peeled and sliced
1 tsp. fresh lemon juice
3 oranges, peel removed (page 14)
1⅓ cups whole wheat flour
3 tsp. baking powder
⅓ cup light brown sugar
3 tbsp. safflower oil
½ tsp. pure vanilla extract
1 tbsp. honey
2 tbsp. fresh orange juice

Preheat the oven to 325° F. Grease an 8-inch round cake pan. Line the bottom of the pan with wax paper and grease the paper.

Sprinkle the pear slices with lemon juice. Cut two of the oranges into segments, discarding the membranes (page 14). From the other orange, cut one slice across the grain of the segments. Put this slice in the middle of the prepared pan. Alternate the orange segments and pear slices around the perimeter of the pan, to cover the base.

Sift the flour and baking powder into a bowl, then stir in the sugar. Whisk the oil with the vanilla extract and ⅔ cup of cold water until well blended. Make a well in the center of the dry ingredients and stir in the oil mixture. Beat well with a wooden spoon until the batter is smooth and glossy.

Pour the batter over the fruit in the pan and level the top. Bake the cake in the center of the oven until well risen, lightly browned, and springy when touched in the middle—40 to 45 minutes.

Leave the cake in the pan for five minutes, then loosen the edge with a knife. Turn the cake out onto a wire rack and remove the lining paper. Let it cool.

Heat the honey and orange juice in a small saucepan, stirring to blend the mixture. Boil the liquid for about 30 seconds, until it is syrupy. Quickly brush the oranges and pears with the glaze.

Pineapple Cake

THE PINEAPPLE MAKES THIS CAKE VERY MOIST. AS A RESULT, THE
CURRANTS DO NOT REMAIN DISTRIBUTED THROUGHOUT THE BATTER
BUT FORM A LAYER AT THE BOTTOM OF THE CAKE.

Serves 12
Working time: about 25 minutes
Total time: about 3 hours

Calories **220**
Protein **4g.**
Cholesterol **40mg.**
Total fat **10g.**
Saturated fat **2g.**
Sodium **95mg.**

½ cup polyunsaturated margarine
⅔ cup light brown sugar
2 eggs
1¾ cups all-purpose flour
1¾ tsp. baking powder
1 cup currants
½ lb. fresh pineapple

Preheat the oven to 325° F. Line an 8-inch round cake pan with wax paper and grease the paper.

Using a wooden spoon, cream the margarine and sugar together until light and fluffy. Beat in the eggs one at a time, following each with 1 tablespoon of the flour. Sift in the remaining flour, together with the baking powder. With a metal spoon or rubber spatula, fold in the flour mixture, followed by the currants. Puree the pineapple in a food processor or blender, and fold it into the cake mixture.

Turn the mixture into the prepared pan and level the top. Bake the pineapple cake for about one and a quarter hours, until it is firm to the touch and golden brown. Leave the cake in the pan for 10 minutes, then turn it out onto a wire rack and let it cool before removing the lining paper.

SUGGESTED ACCOMPANIMENT: *sliced fresh pineapple.*

Plum Pizza

Serves 10
Working time: about 45 minutes
Total time: about 2 hours and 30 minutes

Calories **240**	⅓ cup nonfat dry milk
Protein **7g.**	⅓ cup low-fat ricotta cheese
Cholesterol **105mg.**	⅓ cup plain low-fat yogurt
Total fat **8g.**	2 tbsp. honey
Saturated fat **3g.**	1 tsp. ground cinnamon
Sodium **35mg.**	1½ lb. red plums, pitted and quartered
	2 tbsp. apricot jam without added sugar

Yeast dough

1 cake (.6 oz.) fresh yeast, or
1 envelope (¼ oz.) active dry yeast
6 tbsp. scalded, tepid milk
2 tbsp. sugar
2 cups bread flour
⅛ tsp. salt
2 tbsp. unsalted butter, melted
1 egg, beaten

To make the dough, mix the yeast with the tepid milk, the sugar, and 1 tablespoon of the bread flour. Leave the yeast liquid in a warm place for 10 to 15 minutes, until it froths. Mix the liquid with the salt, butter, egg, and remaining flour, and knead the dough on a lightly floured surface for five minutes. Put the dough in an oiled bowl, cover it with oiled plastic wrap, and let it rise for about one hour, until the dough has doubled in volume.

Meanwhile, preheat the oven to 400° F. Beat the powdered milk, ricotta cheese, yogurt, honey, and cinnamon together with a wooden spoon. Grease a 10-inch round pan.

On a lightly floured surface, roll out the risen dough until it is approximately the size of the prepared pan. Press the dough against the pan's base and sides.

Spread the cheese mixture over the dough and arrange the plums on the top, cut side down. Bake the pizza for about 30 minutes, until the dough is golden brown and the plums are tender.

Let the pizza cool for 15 minutes, then warm the jam in a small saucepan and brush it over the plums. Serve the pizza warm.

EDITOR'S NOTE: *Instead of plums, the pizza can be made with peaches, apricots, or thinly sliced apples or pears.*

Banana Layer Cake

Serves 12
Working time: about 30 minutes
Total time: about 2 hours

Calories **235**
Protein **5g.**
Cholesterol **45mg.**
Total fat **11g.**
Saturated fat **2g.**
Sodium **70mg.**

⅓ cup brown sugar
6 tbsp. safflower oil
2 eggs
3 bananas, peeled and mashed
1 tsp. finely grated lemon zest
1⅓ cups whole wheat flour
1½ tsp. baking powder
¼ tsp. ground allspice
¾ cup rolled oats
½ tsp. confectioners' sugar
Yogurt-banana filling
1 cup yogurt cheese (Glossary, page 140)
1 banana, peeled and finely chopped

Preheat the oven to 350° F. Grease a 7-by-11-inch cake pan; line the bottom with wax paper and grease the paper. Whisk together the brown sugar, oil, and eggs until the mixture is thick and pale. Stir in the mashed bananas and lemon zest. Sift the flour with the baking powder and allspice into the banana mixture, adding the bran left in the sieve. Add the oats and then fold the ingredients together with a large spoon. Transfer the batter to the prepared pan and level the surface. Bake the banana cake for about 30 minutes, until risen and firm to the touch. Leave it in the pan for 10 minutes, then transfer it to a wire rack to cool.

Remove the paper and trim the cake's edges. Split the cake in half horizontally, then halve it lengthwise.

To make the filling, mix the yogurt cheese with the chopped banana. Spread one-third of the filling over a layer of cake; place another layer with filling on top, and then repeat for the other two layers. Dust the top of the cake with the confectioners' sugar.

Apple and Date Cake

Serves 14
Working time: about 20 minutes
Total time: about 4 hours

Calories **240**
Protein **5g.**
Cholesterol **50mg.**
Total fat **7g.**
Saturated fat **1g.**
Sodium **100mg.**

2⅓ cups whole wheat flour
3 tsp. baking powder
1 tsp. ground cinnamon
1 tsp. ground ginger
½ tsp. grated nutmeg
⅔ cup dark brown sugar
1⅓ cups dried dates, chopped
1 lb. apples, peeled and cored
⅔ cup cider
3 eggs
⅓ cup safflower oil
2 tbsp. honey

Preheat the oven to 350° F. Grease a deep, 8-inch round cake pan. Line the base with wax paper and grease the paper.

Sift the flour and baking powder into a bowl, adding the bran left in the sieve. Stir in the cinnamon, ginger, nutmeg, sugar, and dates. Grate half the apples and add them to the dry ingredients with the cider, eggs, and oil. With a wooden spoon, beat the mixture thoroughly and transfer it to the prepared pan.

Slice the remaining apples thinly. Place the slices so that they overlap, forming two circles on top of the cake; stand a few slices upright in the center. Bake the cake for one and a quarter to one and a half hours, until a skewer inserted in the center comes out clean.

Turn the cake out onto a wire rack and remove the lining paper. While the cake is still warm, boil the honey for one minute in a small saucepan. Brush the apples with the honey, then let the cake cool.

Apple Cake with Currants

Serves 16
Working time: about 25 minutes
Total time: about 5 hours

Calories **240**
Protein **3g.**
Cholesterol **35mg.**
Total fat **7g.**
Saturated fat **1g.**
Sodium **110mg.**

1⅓ cups all-purpose flour
½ tsp. baking soda
1 tsp. ground cinnamon
½ tsp. ground ginger
1 cup whole wheat flour
½ cup polyunsaturated margarine
⅔ cup light brown sugar
2 eggs
1 tbsp. fresh lemon juice
1¼ cup currants
1 cup golden raisins
½ cup mixed candied peel, chopped
1 lemon, grated zest only
½ lb. apples, peeled, cored, and coarsely grated
2 tbsp. sugar

Preheat the oven to 350° F. Grease an 8-inch round cake pan and line it with parchment paper.

Sift the all-purpose flour into a bowl, together with the baking soda, cinnamon, and ginger. Mix in the whole wheat flour.

In another bowl, cream the margarine and sugar until the mixture is very pale and fluffy. With a wooden spoon, beat in the eggs one at a time, following each with 1 tablespoon of the flour mixture; then add the lemon juice and fold in the remaining flour. Add the currants, golden raisins, mixed peel, lemon zest, and grated apple, and mix all the ingredients together thoroughly.

Spoon the mixture into the prepared pan and level the top. Then sprinkle the sugar evenly over the surface of the cake.

Bake the cake for one and a quarter to one and a half hours, until it is golden brown and firm to the touch. Leave the cake in the pan for 10 minutes, then turn it out onto a wire rack. Let it cool before removing the lining paper.

Harvest Cake

Serves 28
Working time: about 40 minutes
Total time: about 7 hours

Calories **185**
Protein **5g.**
Cholesterol **30mg.**
Total fat **6g.**
Saturated fat **2g.**
Sodium **120mg.**

½ lb. cooking apples, peeled, cored, and chopped
½ lb. pears, peeled, cored, and chopped
½ lb. plums, pitted and chopped
1¼ cups raisins
¾ cup apple or grape juice
1⅓ cups whole wheat flour
¾ cup light brown sugar
¾ cup polyunsaturated margarine
1 tsp. each ground cinnamon, ground ginger
3 eggs
5 cups whole-wheat flakes cereal
Topping
1 green apple
1 pear
1 tbsp. lemon juice
¾ cup yogurt cheese (Glossary, page 140)
1 tbsp. plain low-fat yogurt
1 tsp. honey

Grease an 8-by-10-inch oblong pan. Line it with wax paper and grease the paper. Mix the chopped apples, pears, and plums with the raisins and apple or grape juice in a bowl. Cover and leave them for up to one hour, to plump the fruit.

Preheat the oven to 325° F.

Put the flour, sugar, margarine, spices, and eggs in a mixing bowl. Stir with a wooden spoon and beat the mixture until it is smooth and glossy. Add the soaked fruit and the wheat flakes to the cake mixture a little at a time, stirring well after each addition.

Spoon the mixture into the prepared pan and level the top. Bake in the center of the oven until risen, lightly browned, and springy when touched in the center—one and a half to one and three quarter hours.

Loosen the edges of the cake with a knife, turn it out of the pan onto a wire rack, and remove the lining paper. Let the cake cool completely.

To make the topping, core and thinly slice the apple and pear. Sprinkle the slices with lemon juice to stop discoloration. Put the yogurt cheese in a bowl with the yogurt and honey, and blend them together. Spread the cheese mixture over the top of the cake, and arrange the apples and pears in an alternating pattern down the center.

Zucchini Cake

THE ZUCCHINI IN THIS CAKE SUPPLIES MOISTURE
AND A FLAVOR THAT BLENDS REMARKABLY WELL WITH THE
SWEET INGREDIENTS.

Serves 12
Working time: about 15 minutes
Total time: about 2 hours and 30 minutes

Calories **225**
Protein **4g.**
Cholesterol **25mg.**
Total fat **9g.**
Saturated fat **3g.**
Sodium **155mg.**

½ lb. zucchini, coarsely grated
¾ cup fresh dates, pitted and chopped
½ cup raisins
4 tbsp. honey
½ cup polyunsaturated margarine
⅔ cup light brown sugar
1 egg, beaten
2 cups whole wheat flour
2 tsp. baking powder

Preheat the oven to 325° F. Grease a shallow 9-inch round cake pan. Line its base with wax paper and grease the paper.

Stir the grated zucchini with the dates, raisins, and honey in a mixing bowl. In another bowl, cream the margarine and brown sugar together until light and fluffy. Add the eggs with 2 tablespoons of water, and beat with a wooden spoon until the mixture is smooth and glossy.

Sift the flour with the baking powder, and fold these ingredients into the creamed margarine mixture using a spatula or large spoon. Then fold in the zucchini, dates, and raisins.

Spoon the mixture into the prepared pan and level the top. Bake the cake in the center of the oven until risen, lightly browned, and springy when touched in the middle—55 to 60 minutes.

Loosen the cake from the sides of the pan with a knife. Turn the cake out onto a wire rack and remove the lining paper. Let the cake cool completely.

Pumpkin Cake

Serves 16
Working time: about 20 minutes
Total time: about 3 hours

Calories **170**
Protein **4g.**
Cholesterol **15mg.**
Total fat **9g.**
Saturated fat **3g.**
Sodium **180mg.**

1 lb. fresh pumpkin, peeled and chopped
1⅓ cups whole wheat flour
3 tsp. baking powder
1 tsp. ground cinnamon
1½ cups rolled oats
¼ cup light brown sugar
6 tbsp. polyunsaturated margarine
1 egg, beaten
Honey-cheese topping
1 cup low-fat ricotta
2 tbsp. plain low-fat yogurt
4 tsp. honey
2 tbsp. pumpkin seeds, lightly toasted

Put the pumpkin in a saucepan with 4 tablespoons of water. Bring the water to a boil and simmer for two to three minutes, or until the pumpkin is tender. Strain the pumpkin and puree it in a blender or food processor. You should have at least 1 cup of puree. Allow it to cool.

Preheat the oven to 325° F. Grease an 8-inch-square cake pan. Line it with wax paper and grease the paper.

Sift the flour into a bowl together with the baking powder and cinnamon. Add the oats and sugar, and stir. Rub in the margarine with your fingertips or the back of a wooden spoon until the mixture resembles fine bread crumbs.

Stir in the egg and the cup of pumpkin puree, then beat the mixture with a wooden spoon for one minute, until it is smooth. Spoon the mixture into the prepared pan and level the top.

Bake the cake in the center of the oven until risen, golden brown, and springy when touched in the middle—50 to 60 minutes. Turn the cake out onto a wire rack and remove the lining paper. Let the cake cool completely.

Meanwhile, make the topping: Put the ricotta, yogurt, and honey in a bowl, and beat them with a wooden spoon until smooth. Spread the top and sides of the cake evenly with the topping and score the top with a fork. Press pumpkin seeds against the sides.

EDITOR'S NOTE: *Use store-bought pumpkin seeds: Those from the inside of the pumpkin would be too damp. To toast the seeds, heat them in a heavy skillet, shaking the pan constantly, until the color begins to change—a minute or two.*

Maple Pumpkin Tea Bread

Serves 12
Working time: about 30 minutes
Total time: about 5 hours

Calories **160**
Protein **4g.**
Cholesterol **45mg.**
Total fat **7g.**
Saturated fat **2g.**
Sodium **60mg.**

½ cup safflower oil
½ cup maple syrup
2 eggs
1⅓ cups all-purpose flour
½ tsp. baking soda
½ tsp. ground cinnamon
¼ tsp. ground cloves
¼ tsp. grated nutmeg
¼ tsp. baking powder
1 cup pumpkin puree or canned pumpkin
½ cup raisins
⅔ cup shelled macadamia or Brazil nuts, coarsely chopped

Preheat the oven to 350° F. Grease a 5-by-9-inch loaf pan. Line the bottom of the pan with wax paper and grease the paper.

Whisk the oil, maple syrup, and eggs together in a bowl until pale. Sift the flour into another bowl with the baking soda, cinnamon, cloves, nutmeg, and baking powder. Fold these dry ingredients into the oil mixture and mix in the pumpkin, the raisins, and all but 3 tablespoons of the nuts.

Transfer the mixture to the prepared pan and level the surface. Sprinkle the mixture with the remaining macadamia or Brazil nuts.

Bake the cake for one hour to one and a quarter hours, until risen and firm to the touch. Leave it in the pan for 10 minutes, then turn it out onto a wire rack and allow it to cool completely before removing the lining paper.

EDITOR'S NOTE: *To make the pumpkin puree, remove the seeds from a 1¼-lb. wedge of pumpkin. Wrap the wedge in foil. Bake the pumpkin in a preheated 350° F. oven for 45 minutes. With a spoon, scoop the flesh into a food processor or blender, and process the pumpkin until it is smooth.*

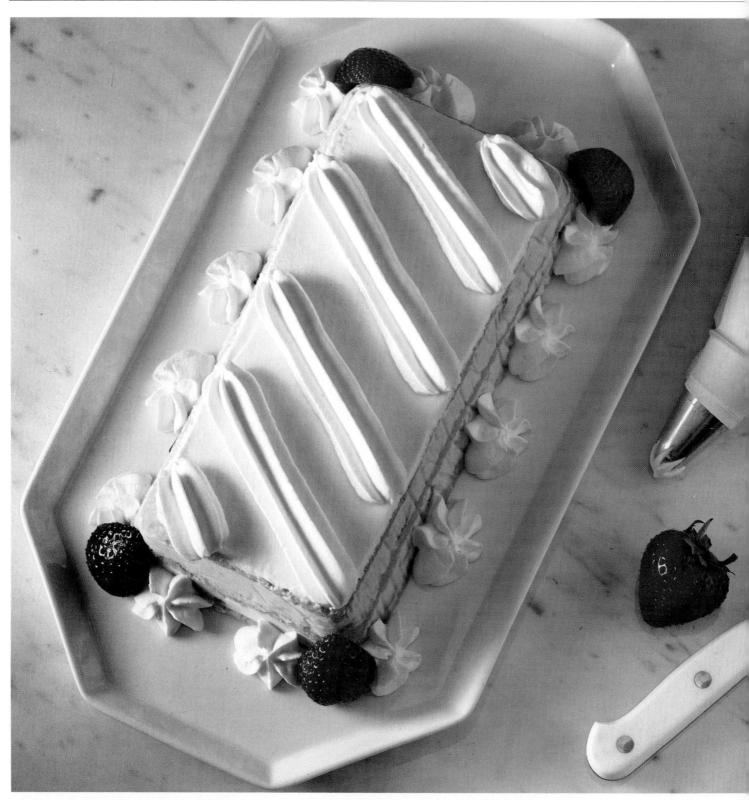

2 *Piped lines of cream adorn a layered sponge cake enlivened with cognac; strawberries will complete the decoration at virtually no calorie cost.*

Stylish Presentations

Tiers of sponge cake and chocolate topped with caramel, a banana cake with lemon butter icing, a rum-flavored savarin bordered with cream—such delights hardly spell austerity. Yet the special-occasion cakes in this chapter are no higher in calories and fat than the others in this book. The secret to the achievement lies in creating most of the decoration with healthful ingredients such as fruit, then using small quantities of cream, butter, nuts, and chocolate where they will be most appreciated.

A pastry bag is a great asset to the health-conscious cook: It turns a mere 2 tablespoons of whipped cream into a scrolled border or a cluster of rosettes. Chocolate curls account for far less fat than a thick chocolate icing, yet look twice as professional. The marzipan ropes topping the fruit cake on page 72 require fewer almonds than would a solid layer. And where the decoration is more lavish, the recipes provide for a basic cake mixture that is not too rich.

Many of the cakes are made from *genoise,* a low-fat sponge cake aerated by whisking eggs and sugar over heat. This mixture, combined with flour, flavorings, and sometimes a little melted butter, bakes to a very light sponge that would be dry on its own but serves as an admirable foundation for assemblies. It can be layered with flavored pastry cream, soaked in liqueur-spiked syrup, and topped with fruit or a film of icing.

Another invaluable base—since it completely lacks fat—is meringue, which is made by whisking sugar into stiffly beaten egg whites. Meringue can be flavored with cocoa, nuts, or a spoonful of fruit puree. It can be piped into such intricate forms as the shell for a Pavlova *(page 91),* or it can be incorporated into a layered assembly such as the hazelnut and raspberry galette on page 92.

Genoise and meringue far from exhaust the scope of this chapter. There are cheesecakes and an ice-cream cake, a strawberry shortcake, and a fruit-packed Christmas garland. As support for the recipes, techniques such as piping, lining pans, and beating eggs and sugar over heat are shown on pages 12 to 19. Inspired by the recipes and guided by the step-by-step demonstrations, you can produce your own variations on the 24 decorative centerpieces in this chapter.

Parsnip and Orange Cake

THE PARSNIP IN THIS RECIPE PROVIDES MOISTURE AND A HINT OF
CRUNCHINESS TO THE CAKE'S TEXTURE; THE DOMINANT
FLAVOR IS ORANGE.

Serves 14
Working time: about 30 minutes
Total time: about 4 hours

Calories **210**
Protein **5g.**
Cholesterol **40mg.**
Total fat **10g.**
Saturated fat **2g.**
Sodium **240mg.**

½ cup polyunsaturated margarine
⅔ cup brown sugar
2 tbsp. barley malt or molasses
1 orange, grated zest and juice only
3 eggs
2⅓ cups whole wheat flour
1 tbsp. baking powder
½ lb. parsnips, peeled and grated
Orange topping
⅓ cup low-fat ricotta cheese
2 tsp. honey
1 orange, zest only, half grated and half julienned and blanched (page 18)

Preheat the oven to 325° F. Grease a deep 8-inch round cake pan. Line the base with wax paper and grease the paper.

Combine the margarine, sugar, barley malt or molasses, and orange zest, and then cream the mixture until it is fluffy. Beat in the eggs one at a time, adding 1 tablespoon of flour with each egg. Sift the rest of the flour with the baking powder, adding the bran remaining in the sieve. Fold the flour, parsnips, and orange juice into the batter.

Turn the batter into the prepared pan. Bake the cake for about one and a quarter hours, until a skewer inserted in the center comes out clean.

Using a knife, loosen the cake from the sides of the pan; turn the cake out onto a wire rack and remove the lining paper. Turn the cake right side up and allow it to cool completely.

To make the topping, blend the ricotta cheese, honey, and grated orange zest together until the mixture is smooth. Spread it over the top of the cake and flute it with a knife or spatula. Sprinkle the orange julienne around the edge of the cake.

Banana Walnut Cake

Serves 14
Working time: about 40 minutes
Total time: about 4 hours

Calories **285**
Protein **4g.**
Cholesterol **25mg.**
Total fat **15g.**
Saturated fat **3g.**
Sodium **25mg.**

1 cup all-purpose flour
4 tsp. baking powder
1 cup whole wheat flour
⅔ cup light brown sugar
⅔ cup walnuts
1 cup finely grated carrots
2 peeled bananas, mashed
1 egg
⅓ cup safflower oil
Lemon butter frosting
3 tbsp. unsalted butter
3 tbsp. low-fat ricotta cheese
¼ tsp. grated lemon zest
⅔ cup confectioners' sugar

Preheat the oven to 350° F. Line an 8-inch-square cake pan with parchment paper.

Sift the all-purpose flour and baking powder into a bowl, and mix in the whole wheat flour and brown sugar. Finely chop ½ cup of the walnuts and stir them in; stir in the carrots. Using a wooden spoon, beat the mashed bananas with the egg and oil in a separate bowl. Make a well in the center of the dry ingredients, add the banana mixture, and beat the batter until it is evenly blended.

Transfer the batter to the prepared pan, level the top, and bake the cake for about one hour, until it is well browned and firm to the touch; a skewer inserted in the center of the cake should come out clean. Turn the cake out onto a wire rack and let it cool with the paper still attached.

To make the lemon butter frosting, beat the butter with a wooden spoon until it is soft, then beat in the ricotta cheese and lemon zest until the mixture is smooth. Sift in enough confectioners' sugar to give the mixture a spreading consistency. Remove the paper from the cake, and turn the cake right side up. Spread the frosting over the top of the cake, swirling it with a round-bladed knife. Break the remaining walnuts into large pieces and sprinkle them over the icing.

Strawberry Ring

Serves 14
Working time: about 30 minutes
Total time: about 2 hours

Calories **120**
Protein **2g.**
Cholesterol **0mg.**
Total fat **3g.**
Saturated fat **0g.**
Sodium **65mg.**

1 cup all-purpose flour
2 tsp. baking powder
½ cup rice flour
½ cup sugar
1 tsp. pure vanilla extract
3 tbsp. safflower oil
4 egg whites
1½ cups strawberries, hulled
1 tsp. arrowroot
¼ cup confectioners' sugar
strawberry leaves to garnish

Preheat the oven to 350° F. Grease and lightly flour a 9-inch springform ring mold—preferably one with a pattern stamped on its base. Sift the flour and baking powder into a mixing bowl. Stir in the rice flour and sugar. In another bowl, whisk the vanilla extract with the oil and 8 tablespoons of water. Stir the liquids into the dry ingredients using a wooden spoon, then beat the mixture to create a smooth batter.

Beat the egg whites in a clean bowl until they are stiff but not dry. With a large spoon, fold one-third of the egg whites into the batter, followed by the remaining egg whites.

Pour the mixture into the prepared mold. Tap the mold against the work surface to level the mixture. Bake the cake in the center of the oven until well risen and springy when touched in the center—20 to 25 minutes. Loosen the edges of the cake with a knife, release the spring, and turn the cake out onto a wire rack. Allow the cake to cool completely.

Rub ¼ cup of the strawberries through a sieve and place them in a small saucepan. Blend the strawberry puree with the arrowroot, then sift in the confectioners' sugar. Bring the puree to a boil, stirring, and simmer it for 30 seconds, until it thickens. Let the puree cool completely.

Thinly slice half of the remaining strawberries and arrange them on the cake's inner edge. Fill the hole in the center of the cake with the whole strawberries, and top them with a few strawberry leaves. Brush the top and sides of the ring with the strawberry puree.

Lime Savarin

Serves 12
Working time: about 1 hour
Total time: about 3 hours and 30 minutes

Calories **255**
Protein **4g.**
Cholesterol **70mg.**
Total fat **10g.**
Saturated fat **5g.**
Sodium **30mg.**

1 cake (.6 oz.) fresh yeast, or 1 envelope (¼ oz.) active dry yeast
5 tbsp. scalded, tepid milk
2 tbsp. sugar
¾ cup bread flour
¾ cup whole wheat flour
⅛ tsp. salt
2 eggs
4 tbsp. unsalted butter, softened
2 limes, freshly grated zest only
1 lime, halved vertically, each half cut into six slices
4 tbsp. apricot jam without added sugar
6 tbsp. whipping cream, whipped
Rum and lime syrup
3 tbsp. fresh lime juice
5 tbsp. honey
2 tbsp. white rum

In a large bowl, mix the fresh yeast with the milk, the sugar, and 1 tablespoon of the bread flour, or reconstitute the dry yeast according to the manufacturer's instructions, combining it with the milk, sugar, and flour. Leave the yeast mixture in a warm place for about 10 minutes, until it is frothy. Add the remaining bread flour to the bowl, together with the whole

wheat flour, salt, eggs, butter, and lime zest. Beat the ingredients together with a wooden spoon.

Grease an 8-inch ring mold and transfer the dough to the mold. Cover the dough with oiled plastic wrap and let it rise in a warm place for 30 to 40 minutes, until the mixture is about ¾ inch from the top of the mold. Meanwhile, preheat the oven to 400° F.

Bake the savarin for 25 to 30 minutes, until it is golden brown and firm to the touch.

While the savarin is cooking, blanch the lime slices to reduce their bitterness: Distribute the slices in a wide, shallow saucepan, pour boiling water over them, bring the water back to a boil, and then drain them. Set the slices aside, and put the lime juice and honey into the pan with 3 tablespoons of water. Bring the syrup to a simmer, place the lime slices back in the pan, and poach them gently for 10 minutes. Remove them from the pan. Bring the syrup to a boil: The hotter it is when it goes on the cake, the more it will soak in. Remove the pan from the heat and add the rum.

Unmold the savarin onto a large plate and immediately spoon the hot syrup over it. Warm the apricot jam in a saucepan. Strain the jam and brush it over the surface of the savarin. Let the savarin cool, then transfer it to a serving plate. Arrange the lime slices around the cake's rim. (For some tastes, the lime is too tart to eat and serves simply as decoration.) Spoon the cream into a large pastry bag fitted with a medium star tip, and pipe shells around the base of the savarin.

Semolina Fruit Cake

Serves 14
Working time: about 30 minutes
Total time: about 4 hours and 30 minutes

Calories **215**
Protein **4g.**
Cholesterol **40mg.**
Total fat **11g.**
Saturated fat **3g.**
Sodium **120mg.**

½ cup polyunsaturated margarine
⅔ cup brown sugar
2 eggs
¾ cup semolina flour
½ cup all-purpose flour
1 tsp. baking powder
2 tbsp. skim milk
½ cup mixed candied peel, chopped
¼ cup hazelnuts, toasted and chopped
1 cup currants
Almond paste
3 tbsp. confectioners' sugar
2 tbsp. granulated sugar
⅓ cup ground almonds
2 tsp. egg white, lightly beaten
½ tsp. lemon juice
½ tsp. unsweetened cocoa powder

Preheat the oven to 350° F. Line an 8-inch-square cake pan with parchment paper.

Cream the margarine and sugar together until the mixture is very pale and fluffy. With a wooden spoon, beat in the eggs one at a time, following each with 1 tablespoon of the semolina flour. Sift the flour with the baking powder, and add them to the mixture with the rest of the semolina and the milk. If necessary, add more milk, a few drops at a time, until the mixture is soft enough to drop easily from a spoon. Fold in the mixed peel, hazelnuts, and currants. Transfer the mixture to the prepared pan and level the top.

Cook the cake for about one hour, until it is firm to the touch and a skewer inserted in the center comes out clean. Leave the cake in the pan for five minutes, then turn it out onto a wire rack and let it cool before removing the lining paper.

To make the almond paste, sift the confectioners' sugar into a bowl, and mix in the granulated sugar and ground almonds. Add the egg white and lemon juice. On a board sprinkled with confectioners' sugar, knead the paste lightly until it is smooth.

Divide the almond paste in half, and knead the cocoa into one of the halves. Roll out both portions of the paste into several long cylinders about ¼ inch in diameter. Twist each brown cylinder with a white one to make a rope. Lay strips of almond rope diagonally across the cake at about 1½-inch intervals, and trim the edges neatly. If the ropes do not stick to the cake by themselves when lightly pressed, attach them with dabs of honey.

EDITOR'S NOTE: *To toast hazelnuts, place them on a baking sheet in a preheated 350° F. oven for 10 minutes.*

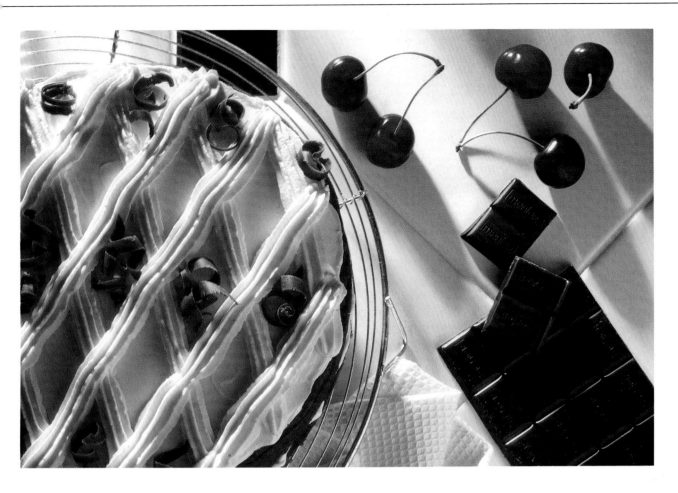

Black-Cherry Chocolate Gateau

Serves 12
Working time: about 50 minutes
Total time: about 3 hours

Calories **140**	
Protein **5g.**	1 lb. black cherries
Cholesterol **60mg.**	1½ tsp. powdered gelatin
Total fat **5g.**	3 eggs
Saturated fat **3g.**	½ cup sugar
Sodium **80mg.**	¾ cup all-purpose flour
	3 tbsp. cocoa powder
	½ tsp. baking powder
	3 tbsp. kirsch or brandy
	¾ cup yogurt cheese (Glossary, page 140)
	5 tbsp. whipping cream
	½ oz. chocolate curls (page 19)

Preheat the oven to 375° F. Grease a round cake pan 8 or 9 inches in diameter; line with parchment paper.

If you wish, set aside 13 or 14 of the best-looking cherries to decorate the cake. Simmer the rest very gently in ⅔ cup of water until very tender but still intact—seven to eight minutes. Strain the liquid into a measuring cup, and if necessary, add water until you have ¾ cup. Put 1 tablespoon of water in a small bowl, and stand it in a pan of gently simmering water. Add the gelatin. When the gelatin has dissolved, stir it into the cherry liquid. Halve the stewed cherries, discard the pits, and add the cherries to the liquid. Let the liquid cool, then refrigerate it until it sets—about two hours.

Meanwhile, put the eggs and all but 2 teaspoons of the sugar in a large bowl over a pan of hot, but not boiling, water. Beat by hand or with an electric mixer until the eggs are thick and very pale. Remove the bowl from the heat, and continue beating until the beater leaves a heavy trail when lifted *(page 12)*. Sift the flour, cocoa, and baking powder together twice, and fold them quickly and evenly through the egg mixture with a mixing spoon. Transfer the batter to the prepared pan and level the top. Cook the sponge cake for 20 to 25 minutes, until it is well risen and firm to the touch. Turn the cake out onto a wire rack, loosen the lining paper but do not remove it, and let the cake cool.

To assemble the gateau, cut the cake in half horizontally, and place the bottom half on a serving plate. Sprinkle it with the kirsch. Mix the yogurt cheese with the remaining sugar, and spread half of it over the cake. Stir the cherry mixture and spread it evenly over the cheese. Top the cherries with the second sponge layer. Spread the remaining cheese mixture on top.

Whip the cream and spoon it into a pastry bag fitted with a small star tip. Pipe a lattice on top of the cake. Place the chocolate curls and reserved cherries in the gaps of the lattice. Chill the cake until serving.

Apricot Tricorn

Serves 12
Working time: about 45 minutes
Total time: about 3 hours

Calories **170**
Protein **4g.**
Cholesterol **70mg.**
Total fat **7g.**
Saturated fat **2g.**
Sodium **60mg.**

3 eggs
⅔ cup sugar
¾ cup all-purpose flour
1 lemon, finely grated zest only
¾ lb. fresh apricots
½ lb. cooking apples, peeled, cored, and sliced
2 tbsp. brandy
⅔ cup yogurt cheese (Glossary, page 140)
6 tbsp. whipping cream
½ cup sliced almonds, lightly toasted

Preheat the oven to 375° F. Grease a rectangular pan approximately 7 by 11 by 1½ inches. Line it with wax paper and grease the paper.

In a bowl set over a pan of hot, but not boiling, water, beat the eggs with 8 tablespoons of the sugar either by hand or with an electric mixer. Remove the bowl from the heat, and continue beating until the eggs are thick and very pale and the beater leaves a heavy trail when lifted *(page 12)*. Sift the flour twice, and fold it quickly and evenly through the mixture, together with the lemon zest. Transfer the batter to the prepared pan and level the top. Bake the cake for 20 to 25 minutes, until well risen and firm to the touch. Turn it out onto a wire rack, loosen the lining paper but do not remove it, and let the cake cool.

For the filling, halve and pit the apricots. Simmer them gently in a wide saucepan in 1 cup of water until they are tender—about 10 minutes. Strain the liquid, remove the apricots' skins, and reserve 10 halves for decorating the gateau. Return the remaining apricots to the pan with the apples and 1 tablespoon of the apricot liquid. Cover the pan and stew the fruit gently until the apples are soft—about five minutes. Add 2 tablespoons of the remaining sugar to the fruit and allow it to cool.

Make two diagonal cuts that connect the midpoint of one of the cake's long sides to the opposite corners, yielding one large triangle and two smaller triangles that together are the same size as the large one. Put the two smaller pieces of cake on a board to form a triangle the same shape as the large piece of cake. Lay the large triangle on top and trim the cakes to exactly the same dimensions. Transfer the two smaller pieces to a serving dish and sprinkle them with brandy. Spread them with the apple and apricot mixture, then top them with the large cake triangle.

Beat the yogurt cheese with the remaining teaspoon or so of sugar. Whip the cream until it is stiff, and fold 2 tablespoons into the cheese mixture. Mask the top and sides of the gateau with the cheese mixture. Press the toasted almonds against the sides. Spoon the remaining cream into a pastry bag fitted with a medium star tip, and pipe a row of shells along two edges of the gateau. Arrange the reserved apricot halves on top, and pipe cream shells along the third border.

EDITOR'S NOTE: *To toast sliced almonds, put them under the broiler for two minutes or until they become golden; turn or shake them constantly.*

Piña Colada Gateau

WITH ITS FLAVORINGS OF COCONUT, PINEAPPLE, AND RUM, THIS
CAKE CONTAINS ALL THE INGREDIENTS OF THE CARIBBEAN
COCKTAIL PIÑA COLADA.

Serves 12
Working time: about 45 minutes
Total time: about 1 hour and 45 minutes

Calories **235**	6 tbsp. unsalted butter
Protein **4g.**	½ cup sugar
Cholesterol **80mg.**	2 eggs, lightly beaten
Total fat **13g.**	¾ cup all-purpose flour
Saturated fat **9g.**	1 tsp. baking powder
Sodium **130mg.**	⅔ cup dried shredded coconut
	Piña colada filling
	2 tbsp. all-purpose flour
	2 tbsp. cornstarch
	2 tbsp. sugar
	1 egg yolk
	1¼ cups skim milk
	¼ pineapple
	1 tbsp. dark rum
	⅓ cup dried shredded coconut

Preheat the oven to 350° F. Grease two 8-inch round
cake pans. Line the bottoms with wax paper and
grease the paper.

To make the cake, cream the butter and sugar in a
large bowl until they are pale and fluffy. Using a wooden spoon, beat the eggs into the creamed butter a little
at a time. Sift the flour and baking powder together
into the egg mixture, and add the coconut. Fold in the
flour and coconut with a large spoon.

Divide the mixture equally between the prepared
pans, and level the surfaces. Bake the cakes for about
20 minutes, until they are risen and firm to the touch.
Turn them out onto a wire rack and let them cool with
the lining paper still attached.

Using a wooden spoon, mix together the flour, cornstarch, sugar, and egg yolk with half of the milk in a
bowl. Bring the remaining milk to a boil in a saucepan,
and pour it over the egg mixture, stirring constantly.
Return the custard to the pan and cook it over gentle
heat, stirring continuously, until it has thickened
enough to form a ribbon. Pour the custard into a bowl
to cool, and place plastic wrap directly on the surface
of the custard to prevent a skin from forming.

Remove the skin and eyes from the pineapple, and
finely chop it. There should be about 1 cup of flesh.

Pour half of the custard from the bowl in which it
has cooled into a second bowl. Add the pineapple to
one bowl of custard and the rum to the other. Remove
the lining paper from the coconut cakes, and make a
sandwich out of them with the pineapple custard in
the middle. Coat the top and sides of the cake with the
rum custard. Scatter shredded coconut evenly over the
custard topping.

Cool Caribbean Cake

Serves 10
Working time: about 40 minutes
Total time: about 5 hours

Calories **180**
Protein **4g.**
Cholesterol **5mg.**
Total fat **5g.**
Saturated fat **2g.**
Sodium **95mg.**

2 oz. semisweet chocolate
2 tsp. honey
1 tbsp. unsalted butter
4 cups wheat flakes cereal
2 tbsp. whipped cream
1 tbsp. dried shredded coconut
Coconut ice cream
½ cup dried shredded coconut, finely chopped
2 tbsp. honey
⅔ cup plain low-fat yogurt
1 egg white
Mango ice cream
2 mangoes, peeled and chopped
4 tbsp. fresh orange juice
2 tbsp. honey
⅔ cup plain low-fat yogurt
1 egg white

Line an 8-inch round cake pan with parchment paper. Fill a small saucepan with water halfway to the top and bring the water to a boil; remove it from the heat. Put the chocolate, honey, and butter in a bowl over the saucepan of hot water. Stir occasionally, until the chocolate and butter have melted. Add the wheat cereal and stir to coat the flakes with the chocolate mixture. Spread the chocolate wheat flakes in the bottom of the prepared pan. Level the layer with the back of a spoon and press it down well. Put the pan in the freezer.

To make the coconut ice cream, put ⅔ cup of water in a small saucepan and bring it to a boil. Remove the water from the heat, and stir in the coconut and honey. Let the mixture cool completely, then stir in the yogurt, and pour the mixture into a shallow plastic container. Place the coconut ice cream in the freezer and leave it until it is firm but not frozen hard—this should take about one hour.

Meanwhile, make the mango ice cream. Puree the mangoes together with the orange juice, honey, and yogurt in a blender or food processor. Pour the puree into a shallow plastic container and place it in the freezer. Leave it until firm but not frozen hard—one to two hours.

Remove the coconut ice cream from the freezer. To break down the crystals, put the ice cream in a bowl and whisk it until smooth, or blend it in a food processor. In a separate bowl, beat the egg white until it is stiff, then whisk the egg white into the ice cream. ▶

Pour the ice cream over the chocolate wheat flakes, and freeze the two layers until firm but not hard.

When the coconut layer is almost set, remove the mango ice cream from the freezer. Put it in a bowl and whisk it until smooth, or blend it in a food processor. In a separate bowl, beat the egg white until it is stiff, then whisk the egg white into the ice cream. Pour the mango ice cream on top of the first two layers, and return the cake to the freezer until frozen—

this process should take approximately two hours.

About 40 minutes before serving the cake, dip the bottom of the pan into warm water for a second, and turn the cake out. Peel off the parchment paper and invert the cake onto a plate. Spoon the whipped cream into a pastry bag fitted with a small star tip. Pipe whirls of cream around the top edge of the cake and decorate the cake with the coconut. Let the cake defrost in the refrigerator for 30 minutes before serving.

Strawberry Shortcake

Serves 10
Working time: about 45 minutes
Total time: about 2 hours and 30 minutes

Calories **220**
Protein **5g.**
Cholesterol **25mg.**
Total fat **11g.**
Saturated fat **4g.**
Sodium **305mg.**

1¼ cups all-purpose flour
½ cup ground almonds
3 tbsp. sugar
1 tbsp. baking powder
3 tbsp. unsalted butter
5 tbsp. buttermilk
2 tbsp. sliced almonds
Strawberry filling
1½ cups strawberries, one reserved, the rest hulled and chopped
4 tbsp. red wine or port
½ cup cottage cheese, sieved
4 tbsp. whipping cream, whipped
1 tbsp. sugar
confectioners' sugar to decorate

Preheat the oven to 400° F. Add the chopped strawberries to the wine and let them macerate.

Sift the flour, ground almonds, sugar, and baking powder together into a bowl. Using your fingertips or the back of a wooden spoon, rub in the butter until the mixture resembles fine bread crumbs. Stir in about 4 tablespoons of the buttermilk—enough to give a soft dough. Knead the dough gently on a lightly floured surface, then press it out to a 7-inch round. Place the round on a nonstick baking sheet.

With a knife, mark the top of the dough into 10 wedge-shaped sections. Brush the top with buttermilk and sprinkle it with the almonds. Bake the shortcake for about 25 minutes, until it is crisp and golden. Turn it out to cool on a wire rack. When the shortcake is cold, split it in half horizontally, and cut the top into the 10 sections.

To make the strawberry filling, mix the cottage cheese with the whipped cream and sugar. Strain the juice from the strawberries and keep it for another use; fold the strawberries into the cream mixture.

Just before serving the cake, spread the strawberry

cream over the bottom of the shortcake. Cover it with the 10 top sections of cake and dust them lightly with confectioners' sugar. Slice the reserved strawberry and arrange the slices in the center of the cake.

Strawberry Cognac Layer Cake

Serves 10
Working time: about 1 hour
Total time: about 10 hours

Calories **175**	
Protein **8g.**	2 eggs
Cholesterol **60mg.**	1 egg white
Total fat **7g.**	½ cup vanilla sugar (Glossary, page 140)
Saturated fat **3g.**	¾ cup all-purpose flour
Sodium **145mg.**	3 tbsp. cognac
	5 tbsp. skim milk
	6 tbsp. whipping cream
	Strawberry filling
	1 cup cottage cheese, sieved
	3 tbsp. skim milk
	2 tbsp. honey
	1 lemon, grated zest only
	1 tbsp. fresh lemon juice
	1½ tsp. powdered gelatin
	1½ cups strawberries, hulled

Preheat the oven to 375° F. Line a loaf pan approximately 4½ by 9 inches and a shallow rectangular pan approximately 9 by 13 inches with parchment paper.

Put the eggs, egg white, and sugar in a bowl set over a pan of gently simmering water. Beat with a hand whisk or an electric mixer until the mixture is very thick and the whisk or beater leaves a heavy trail when lifted *(page 12)*. Remove the mixture from the heat and whisk it until it is cool. Sift the flour twice, and fold it quickly and evenly through the egg mixture. Transfer the batter to the 9-by-13-inch pan and level the top.

Cook the sponge cake for 12 to 15 minutes, until it is well risen and firm to the touch. Turn the cake out onto a wire rack; let it cool and then peel off the paper.

Meanwhile, beat the cottage cheese, skim milk, honey, and lemon zest in a bowl with a wooden spoon. Put the lemon juice in a small bowl and stand it in a pan of gently simmering water, then add the gelatin and let it dissolve. Stir the gelatin into the cheese mixture. Slice half the fruit and add it to the mixture.

Cut lengthwise and across the rectangle of the cake to obtain a piece that fits the base of the loaf pan. Set it in the pan. Combine the cognac and skim milk, and pour 3 tablespoons over the cake in the loaf pan. When the strawberry-cheese mixture begins to thicken, spoon half of it into the loaf pan. Cut a second piece of sponge cake, slightly larger than the first, and use it to cover the strawberry-cheese mixture. Soak the sponge cake with half of the remaining cognac and milk, and spoon in the rest of the strawberry-cheese mixture. From the piece of sponge cake that remains, cut enough to cover the second strawberry-cheese layer. Moisten the cake with the rest of the cognac and milk. Cover the cake with parchment paper and a cardboard rectangle to distribute weight. Set a 1- to 2-lb. weight on the cake and refrigerate it overnight; long chilling will make it firm and easy to slice.

Just before serving the cake, turn it out of the loaf pan and peel off the paper. Whip the cream until stiff, and spread 1 tablespoon over the surface of the cake. Spoon the remaining cream into a pastry bag fitted with a large star tip. Pipe diagonal lines across the top of the cake and stars around the base. Slice or halve the remaining strawberries (depending on their size), and arrange them around the base of the cake and between the lines of cream on the top.

Dobos Torte

NAMED AFTER ITS INVENTOR, JOZSEF C. DOBOS, A FAMOUS
HUNGARIAN PÂTISSIER, THIS CAKE CONSISTS OF LOW-
FAT SPONGE CAKE LAYERED WITH CHOCOLATE PASTRY CREAM
AND TOPPED WITH CARAMEL. TO MAKE THE THIN, DELICATE
SHEETS OF SPONGE CAKE, THE BATTER IS SPREAD OUT ON
PARCHMENT PAPER, AND THE CAKES ARE TRIMMED TO SHAPE
AFTER BAKING. IN THIS VERSION, THE CHOCOLATE
PASTRY CREAM IS CONSIDERABLY LESS RICH THAN IN THE
ORIGINAL CREATION.

Serves 12
Working time: about 1 hour
Total time: about 2 hours and 30 minutes

Calories **175**
Protein **4g.**
Cholesterol **65mg.**
Total fat **5g.**
Saturated fat **2g.**
Sodium **35mg.**

3 eggs
⅔ cup vanilla sugar (Glossary, page 140)
1 cup all-purpose flour
1¼ cups chocolate-flavored pastry cream (page 16)
½ cup sugar
5 tbsp. whipping cream
12 hazelnuts, toasted and skinned

Preheat the oven to 375° F. Draw two 4½-by-10-inch rectangles on each of two sheets of parchment paper. Place the parchment, with marked side down, on a baking sheet.

Put the eggs and sugar in a bowl set over a pan of gently simmering water. Beat the mixture for about 10 minutes with a hand or electric mixer, until the eggs are very thick and creamy, and the beater leaves a heavy trail when lifted *(page 12)*. Remove the bowl from the heat and continue beating the mixture until it is cool. Sift the flour twice, and fold it quickly and

evenly through the egg mixture. Spoon the mixture onto the four marked rectangles and spread it out evenly. Cook the cakes for 10 to 12 minutes, until they are firm and a pale golden brown.

The sponge cakes spread a little during cooking; while they are still warm, trim them with a serrated knife to the dimensions marked on the paper. Transfer the cakes, still on the paper, to a wire rack to cool.

Select the smoothest piece of cake for the torte's top layer, but leave it on the paper. Put the sugar in a small heavy-bottomed saucepan and heat gently, without stirring, until the sugar melts and then turns golden. Pour the caramel quickly over the chosen sponge layer, and spread the caramel with a knife to the edge of the cake. Before the caramel sets, oil a heavy knife, and use it to mark a lengthwise cutting line and six additional lines across the cake, dividing it into 12 portions. Let the caramel harden.

To assemble the Dobos torte, peel one cake layer off the paper and place it on a serving dish. Spread the cake with one-third of the chocolate pastry cream. Cover the chocolate layer with a second layer of cake, more pastry cream, then a third layer of cake, the remaining chocolate pastry cream, and finally the caramel sponge layer. Whip the cream stiffly and spoon it into a pastry bag fitted with a large star tip. Pipe a swirl of cream in the center of each marked portion, and top each cream swirl with a toasted hazelnut. Chill the Dobos torte until it is served.

EDITOR'S NOTE: *To toast and skin hazelnuts, place them on a baking sheet in a preheated 350° F. oven for 10 minutes. Wrap them in a towel and roll them to loosen the skins.*

Layered Chestnut and Orange Gateau

Serves 10
Working time: about 30 minutes
Total time: about 2 hours and 30 minutes

Calories **230**
Protein **5g.**
Cholesterol **50mg.**
Total fat **7g.**
Saturated fat **2g.**
Sodium **100mg.**

1 cup whole wheat flour
1½ tsp. baking powder
⅓ cup light brown sugar
2 tbsp. safflower oil
2 eggs, separated
1 tsp. grated orange zest
⅓ cup hazelnuts, toasted and finely chopped
1 orange, peel with pith sliced off, flesh cut into segments (page 14)
Orange-chestnut filling
2 cups chestnut puree
1 orange, grated zest only
4 tbsp. plain low-fat yogurt
1 tbsp. honey

Preheat the oven to 350° F. Grease a deep 8-inch round cake pan and line its base with wax paper. Grease and lightly flour the paper.

Sift the flour and baking powder together into a mixing bowl, and stir in the sugar. Whisk the oil in a small bowl with the egg yolks, the orange zest, and 3 tablespoons of water. Stir the liquid into the flour mixture, then beat with a wooden spoon to make a smooth, glossy batter.

In another bowl, beat the egg whites until stiff but not dry. Add one-third of the egg whites to the batter, and fold them in, using a spatula or large metal or plastic spoon. Fold in the remaining egg whites and pour the mixture into the prepared pan. Tap the pan on the work surface to level the mixture.

Bake the cake in the center of the oven for 25 to 30 minutes, until well risen, lightly browned, and springy when touched in the center. Loosen the edges of the cake with a knife, and turn it out of the pan onto a wire rack. Remove the wax paper and leave the cake on the rack until it has cooled completely.

To make the orange-chestnut filling, beat the chestnut puree, orange zest, yogurt, and honey with a wooden spoon until smooth. Spoon 2 tablespoons of the filling into a pastry bag fitted with a small star tip.

Cut the cake into three layers. Put the base layer on a plate, and spread its top surface with one-quarter of the remaining filling. Stack and spread the other layers in the same way, and spread the final quarter of the filling over the sides of the cake. Press the chopped hazelnuts against the sides of the cake to coat them evenly. Arrange the orange segments radiating outward from the center of the cake. Pipe stars around the top of the cake and a rosette in the center.

EDITOR'S NOTE: *To obtain 2 cups chestnut puree from fresh chestnuts, slit 2 lb. of nuts down one side, parboil them for one to two minutes, shell, and peel them. Simmer the chestnuts for about 20 minutes in water, until they are tender. Drain and sieve them.*

To toast hazelnuts, put them on a baking sheet in a preheated 350° F. oven for 10 minutes.

Pear and Port Wine Cheesecake

Serves 12
Working time: about 40 minutes
Total time: about 2 hours and 30 minutes

Calories **200**
Protein **4g.**
Cholesterol **35mg.**
Total fat **10g.**
Saturated fat **3g.**
Sodium **195mg.**

1½ cups graham-cracker crumbs
4 tbsp. unsalted butter, melted
1 tsp. ground cinnamon
1 cup part-skim ricotta
⅓ cup sugar
1 tsp. finely grated lemon zest
1 egg
3 large pears
1 tbsp. fresh lemon juice
6 tbsp. port
1 tbsp. currants
1 tsp. arrowroot

Preheat the oven to 350° F. In a bowl, mix the graham-cracker crumbs with the butter and cinnamon. Spread the mixture over the bottom of a 9-inch springform cake pan and press lightly. Bake the crumb base for 15 minutes, then set it aside to cool.

With a wooden spoon, beat together the ricotta cheese, sugar, lemon zest, and egg. Peel and core the pears. Thinly slice them and sprinkle the slices with lemon juice. Cover the crumb base with the cheese mixture, then arrange the pear slices on top in an overlapping pattern. Bake the cheesecake for about 35 minutes, until it is set. Let the cake cool in the pan, then transfer it to a serving plate.

Put the port, currants, and arrowroot in a small pan. Cook them, stirring, over gentle heat for one minute, until the liquid thickens. Let it cool for a minute or two; spoon the mixture over the pears to glaze.

Red-Currant and Blueberry Cheesecake

Serves 12
Working time: about 30 minutes
Total time: about 3 hours

Calories **195**
Protein **7g.**
Cholesterol **30mg.**
Total fat **10g.**
Saturated fat **3g.**
Sodium **180mg.**

2 cups part-skim ricotta cheese
⅔ cup plain low-fat yogurt
2 tbsp. honey
1 tsp. pure vanilla extract
1 egg
1½ cups red currants or raspberries
1½ cups blueberries or blackberries
⅓ cup sugar
4 tsp. arrowroot
Shortcake base
¾ cup whole wheat flour
3 tbsp. whole wheat semolina flour
1 tsp. baking powder
3 tbsp. unsalted butter
1 tbsp. honey

Preheat the oven to 350° F. Grease a 7- or 8-inch-square cake pan with a removable bottom.

To make the shortcake base, sift the flour, semolina, and baking powder in a bowl. Rub in the butter with your fingertips or the back of a wooden spoon until the mixture resembles bread crumbs. Using a fork, stir in the honey and 2 teaspoons of cold water. Knead the dough on a lightly floured surface. Roll it out and then cut it to fit the pan. Lower the dough into the pan and press it well against the base and sides. Prick the dough with a fork and bake it for 10 minutes. Remove it from the oven and reduce the oven temperature to 350° F.

Meanwhile, beat the ricotta cheese, yogurt, honey, and vanilla extract in a mixing bowl with a wooden spoon. Add the egg and beat the mixture until it is smooth. Pour the mixture into the cake pan, then bake the cheesecake until the filling has set—about one hour. Let the cheesecake cool in the pan, then transfer it to a plate.

While the cheesecake cooks, put the red currants and blueberries in separate saucepans, and distribute the sugar between the two pans. Cook the fruit very gently for two minutes, shaking the pans occasionally, until the fruit is softened but still whole. Strain the juice from the blueberries through a nylon sieve. Return the juice to the pan, and put the fruit in a bowl. Strain the red-currant juice through a clean nylon sieve; return the juice to the red-currant pan, and put the red currants in a second bowl.

Blend the arrowroot with 2 tablespoons of water, then stir half into each saucepan. Bring both pans of juice to a boil, stirring, and cook for one minute. Stir the thickened red-currant juice gently into the red currants, and the thickened blueberry juice into the blueberries. Chill the fruit until the cheesecake has cooled. Arrange bands of red currants and blueberries on top of the cheesecake.

EDITOR'S NOTE: *One-half teaspoon of cinnamon or ¼ teaspoon of mace can be added to the dough for the base.*

Apricot-Apple Yogurt Ring

Serves 12
Working time: about 30 minutes
Total time: about 2 hours and 40 minutes

Calories **180**
Protein **8g.**
Cholesterol **0mg.**
Total fat **8g.**
Saturated fat **1g.**
Sodium **20mg.**

2 cups dried apricots
1½ cups peeled, cored, chopped apples or pears
2 cups low-fat plain yogurt
2 tbsp. powdered gelatin
4 fresh apricots, pitted and sliced
Honey-crunch base
2 cups rolled oats
2 tbsp. sesame seeds
2 tbsp. hazelnuts, chopped
4 tbsp. safflower oil
2 tbsp. honey

Put the dried apricots in a saucepan with 1 cup of water. Bring the water to a boil and simmer the apricots, covered, until they are tender—15 to 20 minutes. Puree them in a blender or food processor, then transfer them to a bowl. Simmer the apples in 2 tablespoons of water until tender—eight to 10 minutes. Put the apples through a sieve, adding them to the puree.

Put the yogurt in another bowl and beat in the fruit puree with a wooden spoon. In a small bowl, sprinkle the gelatin over ½ cup of water; stand the bowl in a saucepan of hot water and stir occasionally, until the gelatin has dissolved. Pour the gelatin into the fruit mixture, stirring continuously; beat until the mixture is well blended. Pour the mixture into a 1½-quart ring mold and leave it in a cool place until the gelatin is just beginning to set—about one hour.

To make the honey-crunch base, mix the oats, sesame seeds, and hazelnuts in a bowl. Add the safflower oil and stir well to coat the dry ingredients. Spread the oat mixture in a 9-by-13-inch baking pan and brown it under a broiler for 15 minutes, stirring the cereal once. Heat the honey in a saucepan. When it boils, stir in the oat mixture. Let the cereal cool for five minutes, then spoon it onto the cheesecake's surface; smooth the top with a spatula and press down gently.

Refrigerate the cake until it is firm—about one hour. Dip the mold in hot water to loosen the cheesecake. Cover the mold with the serving plate, invert the cheesecake onto the plate, and remove the mold carefully. Arrange the sliced apricots on top.

Muesli Cheese Tart

Serves 12
Working time: about 30 minutes
Total time: about 2 hours

Calories **170**
Protein **8g.**
Cholesterol **35mg.**
Total fat **8g.**
Saturated **3g.**
Sodium **80mg.**

1½ cups yogurt cheese (Glossary, page 140)
1 tbsp. honey
1 egg
½ tsp. pure vanilla extract
¾ cup plain low-fat yogurt
2 tbsp. toasted and chopped hazelnuts
1 lime, zest only, julienned and blanched (page 18)
Hazelnut muesli base
3 tbsp. honey
2 tbsp. unsalted butter
1 cup rolled oats
¼ cup raisins
1 tbsp. toasted and chopped hazelnuts
1 tbsp. chopped dried apples

Preheat the oven to 325° F. Grease a 4½-by-14-inch plain or fluted tart pan with a removable bottom.

To make the muesli base, heat the honey and butter in a saucepan, stirring occasionally. When the butter has melted, remove the pan from the heat and stir in the oats, raisins, hazelnuts, and dried apples. Spread the muesli mixture over the base of the pan and then level the top with a spatula.

Put the yogurt cheese, honey, egg, and vanilla extract in a mixing bowl with all but 3 tablespoons of the yogurt. Mix the ingredients together with a wooden spoon, then beat them until smooth. Spoon the mixture over the muesli base and level the top with a spatula. Bake the cheesecake in the center of the oven until the filling feels firm when touched in the middle—20 to 25 minutes.

Remove the cake from the oven and spread the remaining yogurt over the top. Return the cake to the oven for five minutes, until the topping has set.

Let the cake cool in the pan. When it reaches room temperature, transfer it to a plate, sprinkle hazelnuts along both sides of the cake, and scatter the lime julienne down the middle.

EDITOR'S NOTE: *To toast hazelnuts, put them on a baking sheet in a preheated 350° F. oven for 10 minutes.*

Valentine Gateau

Serves 12
Working time: about 1 hour
Total time: about 3 hours

Calories **205**
Protein **4g.**
Cholesterol **65mg.**
Total fat **4g.**
Saturated fat **1g.**
Sodium **50mg.**

3 eggs
½ cup sugar
¾ cup all-purpose flour
½ tsp. baking powder
1½ tsp. instant coffee
1 cup pastry cream (page 16)
2 cups fresh raspberries, or frozen raspberries, thawed
4 sugar-frosted rose petals (page 18)
Patterned coffee icing
1 cup, plus 2 tbsp. confectioners' sugar
1 tsp. very strong black coffee
1 oz. semisweet chocolate

Preheat the oven to 375° F. Grease a heart-shaped cake pan approximately 8 inches across at the widest part. Line it with parchment paper.

Using a hand or electric mixer, beat the eggs and sugar together in a bowl set over a pan of simmering water for about 10 minutes—until the mixture is very thick and creamy and the beater leaves a heavy trail when lifted *(page 12)*. Remove the bowl from the heat and beat the mixture until it is cool. Sift the flour, baking powder, and instant coffee together twice, then fold them lightly and evenly through the mixture with a spoon. Transfer the mixture to the prepared pan and level the top. Bake the cake for about 25 minutes, until well risen and firm to the touch. Turn it out onto a wire rack, loosen the lining paper but do not remove it, and allow the cake to cool.

Cut the cake in half horizontally. Spread the lower half with the pastry cream and then cover it with the raspberries. Place the second half of the cake on top.

To make a coffee glacé icing, sift the confectioners' sugar into a bowl, and add the black coffee and about 3 teaspoons of hot water—enough to give a thick, smooth coating consistency. Pour the icing over the top of the gateau and, using a wet spatula, spread it out evenly almost to the edge of the cake. Allow the icing to set.

When the icing is firm, melt the chocolate and spoon it into a wax-paper pastry bag *(page 17)*. Cut off the bag's tip and pipe a lacy line back and forth over the coffee icing. Let the chocolate set. Complete the decoration with the sugar-frosted rose petals.

A Piped Roulade and Its Decoration

MAKING MERINGUE MUSHROOMS. To make the mushroom stalks, pipe 10 pointed rosettes ½ inch in diameter, spaced well apart on the parchment paper. To make the mushroom caps, pipe 10 flatter rosettes 1 inch in diameter.

PIPING THE ROULADE BATTER. Pipe the chocolate-flavored batter in straight lines across the prepared pan. Each line should touch its neighbors, to create a continuous ridged sheet.

Yule Log

YULE-LOG RECIPES USUALLY PRESCRIBE A SPONGE CAKE
ROULADE COVERED WITH CHOCOLATE BUTTER FROSTING. THIS
LOW-FAT VERSION IS CONSTRUCTED FROM A CHOCOLATE-
FLAVORED EGG-WHITE BATTER WITH A CHESTNUT FILLING.

Serves 12
Working time: about 1 hour
Total time: about 2 hours and 30 minutes

Calories **175**
Protein **2g.**
Cholesterol **5mg.**
Total fat **4g.**
Saturated fat **2g.**
Sodium **25mg.**

6 egg whites
2 cups sugar
3 oz. semisweet chocolate, melted and cooled
½ cup all-purpose flour, sifted
cocoa powder to decorate
confectioners' sugar to decorate

Chestnut filling
1 cup chestnut puree
4 tbsp. light cream
1 tbsp. honey

Preheat the oven to 425° F. Place a small piece of
parchment paper on a baking sheet. In addition,
grease a 9-by-13-inch jelly-roll pan and line the pan
with parchment paper. If possible, have ready two
pastry bags fitted with ½-inch plain tips; one, however, will suffice.

Beat the egg whites in a large bowl until they hold
stiff peaks *(page 12)*, then beat in all but 1 tablespoon
of the sugar, 1 tablespoon at a time. To make a crisp
meringue for the mushrooms adorning the log, transfer about 3 tablespoons of the mixture into a smaller ▶

bowl, and whisk in the remaining tablespoon of sugar. Spoon the smaller quantity of meringue into a pastry bag, and pipe mushroom stalks and caps onto the parchment paper on the baking sheet, as shown on page 86. Place the baking sheet on the bottom shelf of the oven.

Return any meringue left in the bag to the bulk of the mixture. Quickly fold in the melted chocolate and the flour with a spoon. Transfer this mixture to the second pastry bag and pipe lines crosswise in the prepared pan, as shown on page 86. Bake the roulade for about 12 minutes, until risen and just firm to the touch. Remove the roulade and turn the oven off, but let the meringue mushrooms cool slowly in the oven.

Turn the roulade out onto a sheet of parchment paper and peel off the lining paper. Loosely replace the lining paper over the sponge cake, cover the cake with the pan, and allow the cake to cool completely.

To make the filling, beat together the chestnut puree, cream, and honey until smooth. Detach the mushrooms from the parchment paper and, using a dab of the chestnut mixture, attach each stalk to a cap.

Uncover the cake and spread it with the filling. Roll up the log carefully, starting at one short end; use the parchment paper to help you. Put the log on a serving plate and arrange the mushrooms on and around it. Dust both log and mushrooms first with cocoa powder and then with confectioners' sugar.

EDITOR'S NOTE: *To obtain 1 cup of chestnut puree from fresh chestnuts, slit 1 lb. of chestnuts down one side, parboil them for one to two minutes, shell, and peel them. Simmer the chestnuts in water for about 20 minutes, until they are tender. Drain and put them through a sieve.*

Christmas Garland

THE SWEETNESS IN THIS CAKE COMES FROM ITS ABUNDANT FRUIT. RICH AND MOIST WHEN FRESH, THIS CAKE WILL, HOWEVER, NOT KEEP AS LONG AS A TRADITIONAL FRUIT CAKE BECAUSE OF THE LACK OF BUTTER OR MARGARINE.

Serves 16
Working time: about 45 minutes
Total time: about 4 hours

Calories **270**
Protein **6g.**
Cholesterol **50mg.**
Fat **11g.**
Saturated fat **2g.**
Sodium **65mg.**

1 orange, finely grated zest and juice
⅔ cup chopped candied cherries
⅓ cup chopped mixed candied peel
3 tbsp. angelica or other green candied fruit, chopped
3 tbsp. candied pineapple, chopped
1 cup dried pears, chopped
½ cup dried apricots, chopped
½ cup golden raisins
½ cup currants
½ cup raisins
¾ cup walnuts, chopped
¾ cup Brazil nuts, chopped
⅓ cup almonds, chopped
1 cup whole wheat flour
¼ tsp. ground cinnamon
¼ tsp. ground allspice
¼ tsp. ground cloves
¼ tsp. grated nutmeg
1 tsp. baking powder
3 eggs, beaten
1 tbsp. molasses
Icing and decoration
1 cup confectioners' sugar
1 tbsp. brandy
8 walnut halves
4 candied cherries, quartered
holly leaves for garnish

Preheat the oven to 300° F. Grease an 8-inch ring mold. Put the orange zest and juice in a large bowl. Stir in the chopped cherries, mixed peel, angelica, pineapple, pears, apricots, golden raisins, currants, raisins, walnuts, Brazil nuts, and almonds. Sift in the flour, cinnamon, allspice, cloves, nutmeg, and baking powder, adding the bran left in the sieve. Pour in the eggs and molasses. Beat the mixture well with a wooden spoon. Transfer it to the greased ring mold and press it down.

Bake it for 45 minutes, or until it feels firm. Leave the cake in the pan for 10 minutes, then invert it onto a wire rack and set it aside until it is completely cool.

To make the icing, mix the confectioners' sugar with the brandy and a little water, if necessary, to give a thin coating consistency. Spoon the icing over the cake, then decorate the cake with the walnut halves, cherry quarters, and holly leaves.

Simnel Cake

A SIMNEL CAKE, TRADITIONALLY SERVED AT EASTER IN
ENGLAND, HAS A CENTRAL LAYER OF MARZIPAN
AND 11 MARZIPAN BALLS ON TOP TO REPRESENT 11 OF JESUS'
12 APOSTLES; JUDAS, THE BETRAYER, IS OMITTED.
IN THIS VERSION OF THE CAKE, THE MARZIPAN IS MADE
WITH HAZELNUTS, WHICH CONTAIN LESS FAT THAN THE MORE
COMMONLY USED ALMONDS.

Serves 16
Working time: about 50 minutes
Total time: about 7 hours and 30 minutes

Calories **325**
Protein **9g.**
Cholesterol **40mg.**
Total fat **4g.**
Saturated fat **3g.**
Sodium **75mg.**

⅔ cup skim milk
⅔ cup fresh orange juice
4 tbsp. unsalted butter
1¼ cups dried apricots, chopped
1¼ cups dried dates, chopped
1¼ cups dried figs, chopped
1 cup golden raisins
1 cup raisins
½ cup currants
1½ cups soy flour
½ tsp. ground cinnamon
¼ tsp. ground cloves
¼ tsp. ground allspice
1 tsp. grated nutmeg
1⅓ cups whole wheat flour
2 eggs, beaten
½ tsp. baking soda
1 tsp. honey
2 tbsp. confectioners' sugar
Hazelnut marzipan
1 cup hazelnuts, ground
½ cup semolina flour
⅔ cup light brown sugar
½ tsp. almond extract
1 egg white

Preheat the oven to 275° F. Grease a deep 8-inch round cake pan. Double-line the pan with wax paper and grease the paper. To protect the outside of the cake from scorching during the long cooking, tie a double thickness of brown paper around the outside of the pan, and place the pan on a baking sheet double-lined with brown paper.

Put the milk, orange juice, and butter in a large saucepan. Bring the mixture to a boil. Add the apricots, dates, figs, golden raisins, raisins, and currants. Stir the fruit well and bring the liquid back to a boil, stirring occasionally. Remove the pan from the heat and let the fruit plump up until it is barely warm.

Meanwhile, make the hazelnut marzipan. Mix the nuts, semolina, sugar, and almond extract in a bowl. Add enough of the egg white to form a soft, pliable dough, and knead the marzipan on a lightly floured board until it is smooth. Then cover the board with a large sheet of plastic wrap. Roll out one-third of the marzipan on the plastic wrap and trim the marzipan to an 8-inch round.

Sift the soy flour into a large bowl with the cinnamon, cloves, allspice, and nutmeg. Add the whole wheat flour. When the fruit in the saucepan has cooled, add the eggs and baking soda to the pan and stir well. Gradually stir the fruit into the flour mixture with a wooden spoon.

Spoon half of the cake batter into the prepared pan and level the top with a spatula. Pick up the plastic wrap with the marzipan and invert the marzipan onto the batter; spread the remaining cake batter over the marzipan and level the top with a spatula.

Bake the cake in the center of the oven until it is risen and dark brown—this should take two to two-and-a-half hours. Test the cake by inserting a warm skewer into its center. If the skewer is clean when removed, the cake is cooked; otherwise, return the cake to the oven and test at 15-minute intervals. Let the cake cool in the pan, then turn it out and remove the lining paper.

From the unused marzipan make 11 balls about 1 inch in diameter. Roll the remaining marzipan on the plastic wrap into a round to fit the top of the cake. Brush the top of the cake with the honey and set the marzipan in position. Flute the edge by pinching it with a thumb and forefinger. Arrange the 11 balls around the edge of the cake, attaching each of them with a dab of honey.

To flavor the marzipan and cook the semolina, place the cake under the broiler, 4 to 6 inches from the heat, until the marzipan is lightly browned—about two minutes. Let the marzipan cool.

Sift the confectioners' sugar into a small bowl. Mix in 2 teaspoons of water and beat until the icing is smooth. Pour the icing over the center of the cake. Allow the simnel cake to sit for at least four hours before serving.

EDITOR'S NOTE: *For a light-colored marzipan, use granulated sugar in place of brown sugar.*

Golden Passion Pavlova

A CONFECTION OF MERINGUE AND FRUIT, PAVLOVA WAS CREATED IN 1935 BY AN AUSTRALIAN CHEF AND NAMED IN HONOR OF THE GREAT RUSSIAN BALLERINA, WHO HAD RECENTLY TOURED AUSTRALIA. HERE, THE TRADITIONAL CREAM FILLING IS REPLACED WITH YOGURT CHEESE.

Serves 10
Working time: about 25 minutes
Total time: about 2 hours and 40 minutes

Calories **90**
Protein **3g.**
Cholesterol **25mg.**
Total fat **3g.**
Saturated fat **2g.**
Sodium **95mg.**

2 tsp. cornstarch
1 tsp. vinegar
½ tsp. pure vanilla extract
3 egg whites
⅛ tsp. cream of tartar
⅔ cup light brown sugar
Passion cream filling
1 cup yogurt cheese (Glossary, page 140)
2 tsp. honey
2 passion fruit
2 kiwi fruit, peeled and sliced
1 mango, peeled and chopped

Preheat the oven to 275° F. Line a baking sheet with parchment paper. Draw an 8-inch circle on the paper in pencil, then turn the paper over.

Blend together the cornstarch, vinegar, and vanilla extract in a small bowl. Beat the egg whites and cream of tartar in a large bowl until the whites stand in stiff peaks *(page 12)*. Add a quarter of the sugar at a time to the whites, beating well after each addition. Spoon in the cornstarch mixture and beat until the meringue is glossy and thick enough to hold soft peaks.

Transfer the meringue to a large pastry bag fitted with a medium star tip. Pipe a series of swirls around the outside of the marked circle on the paper. Pipe two-thirds of the remaining meringue within the circle. Smooth the meringue with a spatula and make sure there are no gaps. With the remaining meringue, pipe a second series of swirls on top of the first ones to create a raised border.

Bake the Pavlova in the center of the oven for one hour. Turn off the heat, open the oven door, leave the oven door ajar, and let the Pavlova cool slowly. It will take about another hour.

To make the passion cream filling, mix the yogurt cheese and honey in a bowl with a wooden spoon, then beat them until smooth. Put ⅓ cup of the filling into a nylon pastry bag fitted with a medium star tip. Halve the passion fruit. Scoop out the flesh with a teaspoon and stir it into the remaining filling.

Carefully peel the paper away from the meringue and place the meringue on a flat plate. With the filling in the pastry bag, pipe a circle of swirls just inside the raised meringue border. Spread the passion cream filling inside the swirls. Cover the filling with the kiwi fruit slices and chopped mango.

EDITOR'S NOTE: *The meringue can be cooked in advance and stored for up to a week in an airtight container.*

Hazelnut and Raspberry Galette

Serves 12
Working time: about 1 hour
Total time: about 2 hours

Calories **165**
Protein **5g.**
Cholesterol **65mg.**
Total fat **8g.**
Saturated fat. **3g.**
Sodium **70mg.**

3 eggs
2 tbsp. sugar
¼ cup whole wheat flour
½ tsp. pure vanilla extract
1 cup plain yogurt
2 cups fresh raspberries, or frozen raspberries, thawed
4 tbsp. whipping cream, whipped
Hazelnut meringue
3 egg whites
⅛ tsp. salt
½ cup sugar
¾ cup hazelnuts, toasted, skinned, and finely chopped
1 tbsp. cornstarch

Preheat the oven to 400° F. Grease two 9-by-13-inch jelly-roll pans. Line them with parchment paper and lightly grease the paper.

To make the hazelnut meringue, use a whisk or an electric mixer to beat the egg whites with the salt until the mixture stands in stiff peaks *(page 12)*, then gradually beat in the sugar 1 tablespoon at a time, beating well between each addition. Mix the hazelnuts with the cornstarch and fold them into the meringue. Spread the meringue evenly in one of the prepared pans and bake it for 20 minutes. Let it cool in the pan. Reduce the oven to 350° F.

Beat the eggs and sugar over a pan of simmering water until they are pale and thick *(page 12)*. Remove the mixture from the heat and beat it until cool. Fold in the flour and vanilla extract. Transfer the mixture to the second pan and level the surface. Bake the sponge cake for about 15 minutes, until just firm to the touch. Let it cool in the pan.

Remove the sponge cake and the meringue from their pans. Trim them to the same size. Cut both the meringue and the sponge cake in half lengthwise. Crumble the meringue trimmings and stir them into the yogurt. Spread the yogurt over one layer of meringue and both layers of cake.

Reserve 30 raspberries, then divide the remainder between the three layers spread with yogurt. Assemble the galette, placing a sponge-cake layer at the bottom and covering it with the decorated meringue layer, the second sponge layer, and finally the remaining meringue layer. Press the top layer down gently. Using a medium star tip, pipe lines of cream across the galette. Arrange rows of raspberries between the lines.

EDITOR'S NOTE: *To toast and skin hazelnuts, place them on a baking sheet in a preheated 350° F. oven for 10 minutes. Wrap them in a towel and rub briskly to loosen the skins. Strawberries can be used instead of raspberries.*

Meringue Coffee Torte

Serves 12
Working time: about 50 minutes
Total time: about 2 hours and 30 minutes

Calories **165**
Protein **10g.**
Cholesterol **45mg.**
Total fat **6g.**
Saturated fat **1g.**
Sodium **220mg.**

2 tbsp. light brown sugar
2 eggs
½ cup whole wheat flour
½ tsp. baking powder
1¼ cups yogurt cheese (Glossary, page 140)
4 tbsp. whipping cream
1 tbsp. honey
3 tsp. strong black coffee
18 walnut halves
confectioners' sugar to decorate
Walnut meringue
2 egg whites
⅓ cup light brown sugar
⅓ cup walnuts, finely chopped
2 tsp. cornstarch

Preheat the oven to 350° F. Grease an 8-inch round cake pan. Line the bottom with wax paper and then grease the paper.

Put the brown sugar and eggs in a bowl set over simmering water. Beat the mixture by hand or with an electric mixer until it is thick and pale *(page 12)*. Remove the bowl from the heat and beat until the beater, when lifted, leaves a trail on the surface. Sift the flour and baking powder together over the mixture. Using a spatula or large metal or plastic spoon, fold in the flour. Pour the mixture into the prepared pan and level the top with a small spatula.

Bake the cake in the center of the oven until risen, lightly colored, and springy when touched in the middle—15 to 20 minutes. Leave the cake in the pan for five minutes, then turn it out onto a wire rack. Remove the paper and let the cake cool.

To make the walnut meringue, reduce the oven setting to 250° F. Line a baking sheet with parchment paper. Draw two 7½-inch circles on the parchment and invert the parchment. (The meringue circles are smaller than the pan in which the cake bakes because meringue, unlike sponge cake, does not shrink as it cools.) In a large bowl, beat the egg whites until they hold stiff peaks *(page 12)*. Add one-third of the sugar at a time, beating well after each addition. Mix together the chopped walnuts and cornstarch, and fold them into the meringue.

Divide the walnut meringue between the two circles and spread it evenly. Bake the rounds for one hour to one hour and 20 minutes, until the meringue feels firm and no longer sticky. Transfer the parchment with the meringue rounds to a wire rack. When the meringue is cold, peel off the parchment.

Beat the cheese and cream in a bowl with a wooden spoon. Stir in the honey and coffee. Put ¼ cup of the coffee cream in a pastry bag fitted with a medium-size star tip.

Place a meringue round on a plate and spread it with one-third of the remaining coffee cream. Slice the cake in half horizontally. Place one layer on the meringue and spread it with another third of the coffee cream. Top the coffee cream with the remaining layer of cake, the rest of the coffee cream, and finally the second meringue round.

Dust the torte with the confectioners' sugar. Pipe scrolls around the top edge of the torte and decorate it with the walnut halves.

3 *A sprinkling of sugar provides the finishing touch for madeleines—scallop-shaped mouthfuls of golden sponge cake.*

Small-Scale Delights

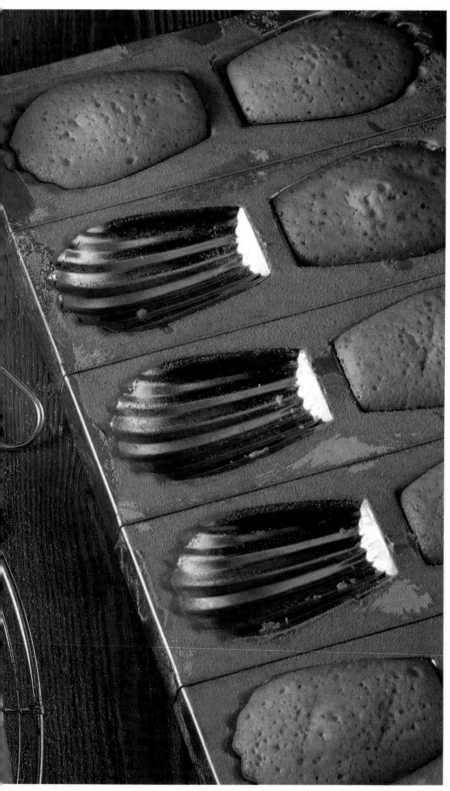

Cooked rapidly and cooled in minutes instead of hours, small cakes provide all the pleasures of home baking without the delay in gratification. Their miniature form does not limit the cook's scope: The range of recipes in this chapter reflects both the plain cakes of chapter 1 and the fancy cakes of chapter 2.

Perhaps the small cakes that are the simplest to make are the bar cakes, in which a mixture is spread out in a shallow pan and sliced into individual squares, bars, or triangles after baking. (Instructions for lining pans appear on page 13.) Many of the bar-cake recipes in this chapter are for robust mixtures of whole grain, dried fruit, and nuts.

The small cakes that are individually shaped before baking take the shortest time of all to cook. Some of those presented on pages 104 to 116 are formed into rounds or crescents by hand, others are stamped with a cutter into shapes that cook individually on a baking sheet, yet others are poured into trays with individual depressions. Fluted and ridged molds, such as the madeleine pan pictured at left, shape the contours of the batter with very decorative results.

Most of the assemblages on pages 116 to 125 start out like bar cakes, with the mixture baked in a shallow pan. But the character of these assembled cakes is very different, for they are based not on whole-grain ingredients but on a feather-light, low-fat sponge cake. Instead of being simply sliced after cooking, the sponge cake is sometimes split horizontally and made into a sandwich with fruit puree or lemon curd in the middle; it may be shaped with cutters into rounds, ovals, or stars and coated with cream, nuts, chocolate, or marzipan. The result is a collection of exquisite morsels that certainly compensate for the time spent in constructing them.

Date and Apricot Triangles

HAZELNUT PASTE CONTAINS LESS FAT AND FEWER CALORIES
THAN THE MORE COMMONLY MADE ALMOND PASTE.

Serves 24
Working time: about 40 minutes
Total time: about 2 hours and 40 minutes

Calories **200**
Protein **3g.**
Cholesterol **30mg.**
Total fat **8g.**
Saturated fat **2g.**
Sodium **60mg.**

2 cups dried apricots, chopped
1¼ cups dried dates, chopped
1 cup raisins
3 tbsp. barley malt
½ cup polyunsaturated margarine
⅔ cup dark brown sugar
3 large eggs
1½ cups whole wheat flour
1 tsp. ground cinnamon
½ tsp. grated nutmeg
1 tbsp. apricot jam without added sugar
Hazelnut paste
1¼ cups hazelnuts, skinned and ground
¾ cup sugar
½ cup rice flour
1 large egg white
2 tsp. rose water

Preheat the oven to 325° F. Grease a 7-by-11-inch baking pan. Line it with wax paper and grease the paper. Cover the apricots with boiling water; let them soak for 30 minutes and then drain them.

Put the apricots, dates, and raisins in a bowl and stir in the barley malt. Beat the margarine and brown sugar with a wooden spoon until the mixture is fluffy, then beat in the eggs one at a time, adding a little flour with each egg. Mix in the remaining flour, the spices, and the fruits.

Transfer the batter to the baking pan and smooth it to the pan's edges. Bake the cake for 30 minutes, then reduce the heat to 300° F. and cook for another 40 minutes, until the mixture is firm in the center. Loosen the cake from the pan and turn it out onto a wire rack to cool. Remove the lining paper.

For the hazelnut paste, mix the hazelnuts, sugar, and rice flour together. Make a well in the center and add the egg white and rose water; stir until the mixture adheres to itself when pressed; if necessary, add more rose water by the ½ teaspoon.

Heat the jam with ½ tablespoon of water, then put the jam through a sieve. Brush it over the base of the cake while it is still warm. Put the paste between sheets of wax paper and roll it into a rectangle to fit the cake.

Drape the paste over the rolling pin and transfer it to the cake. Smooth the edges, then score the paste with a sharp knife to make a lattice pattern. Put the cake under a preheated broiler, 4 to 6 inches from the heat, for one to two minutes, until the paste is tinged with brown. Cut the cake into triangles to serve.

EDITOR'S NOTE: *To skin hazelnuts, first loosen their skins by roasting them on a baking sheet in a 350° F. oven for 10 minutes. Wrap the nuts in a towel and rub them to loosen the skins. Grind the nuts in a rotary grinder or a food processor; a rotary grinder is preferable because it gives a uniform texture without drawing the oil out of the nuts.*

Honey Squares

Serves 24
Working time: about 30 minutes
Total time: about 1 hour and 40 minutes

Calories **160**
Protein **3g.**
Cholesterol **5mg.**
Total fat **8g.**
Saturated fat **1g.**
Sodium **85mg.**

2 cups all-purpose flour
3 tsp. baking powder
1 cup whole wheat flour
2 lemons, finely grated zest only
½ cup, plus 1 tbsp. honey
4 tbsp. unsalted butter
6 tbsp. safflower oil
¼ cup dark brown sugar
1 egg
1 egg white
6 tbsp. buttermilk
6 tbsp. skim milk
24 blanched almonds, split and lightly toasted
6 candied cherries, quartered
1 tbsp. angelica or other green candied fruit, cut into leaf shapes

Preheat the oven to 350° F. Grease a rectangular baking pan that measures 8 by 12 by 1¼ inches and line it with parchment paper.

Sift the all-purpose flour and baking powder into a bowl; mix in the whole wheat flour and lemon zest, and make a well in the center.

Reserving 1 tablespoon of honey, put the remainder into a saucepan with the butter, oil, and sugar. Heat gently until the butter is melted. Let the mixture cool slightly. Very lightly whisk the egg and the egg white together, then whisk in the buttermilk and skim milk. Pour the honey and egg mixtures into the center of the flour. Stir well, then pour the batter into the prepared pan, spreading it evenly.

Bake the honey cake for 35 to 40 minutes, until it is well risen, firm, and springy to the touch. Remove it from the oven and immediately brush the top with the reserved honey. Arrange the nuts, cherries, and angelica leaves on the cake. Cut it into squares when it has cooled.

Coconut Bars

Serves 20
Working time: about 25 minutes
Total time: about 1 hour and 45 minutes

Calories **100**
Protein **2g.**
Cholesterol **36mg.**
Total fat **4g.**
Saturated fat **3g.**
Sodium **18mg.**

3 eggs, separated
⅔ cup sugar
½ lemon, grated zest and juice
⅓ cup semolina flour
3 tbsp. ground almonds
Chewy coconut topping
2 egg whites
½ cup light brown sugar
½ cup dried shredded coconut

Preheat the oven to 350° F. Grease a 7-by-11-inch baking pan, line the bottom with wax paper, and then grease the paper.

Cream the egg yolks together with the sugar, lemon zest, and juice until the mixture is thick. Stir in the semolina and ground almonds. Beat the egg whites until they are stiff, then fold them into the creamed mixture. Transfer the batter into the baking pan and level the batter's surface.

To make the topping, beat the egg whites until they are stiff, then fold in the brown sugar and coconut. Lay teaspoonfuls of the topping at regular intervals on top of the cake. (Large spoonfuls would sink down into the light sponge mixture.) With a fork, carefully spread the topping into an even layer that reaches the pan's edge.

Bake the coconut cake for 35 to 40 minutes, until golden. Turn out the cake onto a rack; the coconut topping will be quite firm and will not crumble. Remove the lining paper, then invert the cake again onto a second rack. When the cake is cool, cut it into bars with a sharp serrated knife.

Fig Bars

Serves 18
Working time: about 25 minutes
Total time: about 2 hours

Calories **145**
Protein **3g.**
Cholesterol **0mg.**
Total fat **9g.**
Saturated fat **2g.**
Sodium **85mg.**

2 cups dried figs, finely chopped
5 tbsp. apple juice
1¼ cups whole wheat flour
⅔ cup polyunsaturated margarine
1½ cups rolled oats
¼ cup light brown sugar
2 tbsp. sesame seeds, toasted

Preheat the oven to 375° F. Grease an 8-inch-square baking pan and line it with wax paper.

Put the dried figs in a saucepan with the apple juice and simmer for five minutes, stirring occasionally, until the fruit is soft. Set the pan aside. In a bowl, blend the flour and margarine together with a fork. Add the rolled oats, sugar, and sesame seeds; using your fingers or the back of a wooden spoon, rub the mixture until it resembles coarse bread crumbs.

Press half of the oat mixture into the pan. Spread the figs and apple juice over it, then sprinkle the remaining oat mixture on top. Press the top oat layer down firmly with a spatula. Bake the fig cake for 40 to 50 minutes, until the top is golden.

Cut the cake into bars while still warm, but leave them in the pan until completely cool.

SUGGESTED ACCOMPANIMENT: *chilled apple juice.*

EDITOR'S NOTE: To toast seeds, sprinkle a layer in a heavy skillet, cover, and cook over high heat. When they begin to pop, heat for 1 minute more, shaking the pan constantly.

Apple Streusel Slices

Serves 20
Working time: about 40 minutes
Total time: about 2 hours

Calories **135**
Protein **2g.**
Cholesterol **0mg.**
Total fat **5g.**
Saturated fat **1g.**
Sodium **55mg.**

5 tbsp. polyunsaturated margarine
1⅔ cups whole wheat flour
1½ lbs. apples, peeled, cored, and chopped
¼ cup dark brown sugar
2 tsp. ground cinnamon
⅔ cup golden raisins
Sesame streusel
3 tbsp. polyunsaturated margarine
⅔ cup whole wheat flour
2 tbsp. light or dark brown sugar
1½ tbsp. sesame seeds
1 tsp. ground cinnamon

In a bowl, rub the margarine into the flour with your fingertips or the back of a wooden spoon until the mixture resembles bread crumbs. Stir in 3 to 4 tablespoons of ice water—enough to make a fairly firm dough—and knead lightly until the dough is smooth. Wrap it in plastic and let it rest for 10 minutes.

Roll out the dough into a thin layer on a lightly floured surface and use it to line a 9-by-13-inch baking pan. Prick the dough with a fork and refrigerate it for 15 minutes.

Meanwhile, preheat the oven to 400° F. Mix the apples with the sugar, cinnamon, and golden raisins.

To make the sesame streusel, rub the margarine into the flour in a bowl until the mixture resembles bread crumbs. Stir in the sugar, sesame seeds, and cinnamon. Sprinkle 3 tablespoons of this mixture over the dough in the pan so that the juice from the apples will be absorbed. Spread the apple mixture in the pan. Distribute the remaining streusel over the apples. Bake the cake for 30 to 35 minutes, until the streusel is golden brown. Cut the apple streusel into slices when it has cooled.

Lemon Semolina Squares

Serves 15
Working time: about 30 minutes
Total time: about 2 hours

Calories **150**	6 tbsp. polyunsaturated margarine
Protein **3g.**	⅔ cup sugar
Cholesterol **30mg.**	1 lemon, grated zest, and juice
Total fat **7g.**	1¼ cups whole wheat flour
Saturated fat **2g.**	2 tsp. baking powder
Sodium **100mg.**	2 large eggs
	½ cup semolina flour
	¼ cup ground almonds
	⅔ cup plain low-fat yogurt
	1 tbsp. pine nuts
	4 tbsp. honey

Preheat the oven to 350° F. Grease a 7-by-11-inch baking pan.

Cream the margarine and sugar together with the lemon zest until the mixture is light and fluffy. Sift the flour with the baking powder, adding any bran left in the sieve. Beat the eggs one at a time into the creamed margarine and sugar; include 1 tablespoon of the flour mixture with the second egg. Fold in the remaining flour and baking powder, then add the semolina flour, almonds, and yogurt.

Transfer the batter into the baking pan and spread the mixture evenly to the edges. Sprinkle the pine nuts over the top and press them gently into the batter. Bake for 40 minutes, or until the cake springs back when pressed in the center.

Make a syrup by heating the honey with ½ cup of water in a small pan. Boil the syrup for one minute, then stir in the lemon juice.

When the sponge cake is done, prick it all over with a fork and slowly pour the warm syrup over it. Let the cake absorb the syrup. When the cake has cooled, cut it into squares and remove them from the pan.

Almond-Apricot Fingers

Serves 18
Working time: about 30 minutes
Total time: about 2 hours

Calories **150**
Protein **3g.**
Cholesterol **25mg.**
Total fat **9g.**
Saturated fat **2g.**
Sodium **100mg.**

1 cup whole wheat flour
2 tsp. baking powder
½ cup polyunsaturated margarine
6 tbsp. light brown sugar
2 eggs
1⅓ cups dried apricots, chopped and soaked for 30 minutes in boiling water
½ cup ground almonds
½ tsp. almond extract
⅓ cup sliced almonds

Preheat the oven to 375° F. Line the bottom of a 9-by-13-inch baking pan with paper.

Sift the flour with the baking powder, adding any bran left in the sieve. Cream the margarine and sugar together until fluffy. Beat in the eggs one at a time, adding 1 tablespoon of the flour mixture with each.

Drain the apricots thoroughly, reserving 1 tablespoon of the juice. Stir the apricots into the batter and fold in the remaining flour mixture, ground almonds, almond extract, and reserved juice. Transfer the mixture into the baking pan. Spread it evenly to the edges and sprinkle it with the sliced almonds.

Bake the cake for 30 to 35 minutes, until it springs back when pressed in the center. Turn out the cake onto a wire rack, remove the paper, and then invert it onto another rack to cool. Cut the cake into fingers when it has cooled.

Hazelnut-Pineapple Slices

Serves 12
Working time: about 30 minutes
Total time: about 3 hours and 30 minutes

Calories **185**
Protein **4g.**
Cholesterol **0mg.**
Total fat **6g.**
Saturated fat **1g.**
Sodium **15mg.**

1½ cups all-purpose flour
⅛ tsp. salt
2 tbsp. light brown sugar
½ tsp. ground cinnamon
1 orange, finely grated zest only
2 tbsp. unsalted butter
1 cake (.6 oz.) fresh yeast, or 1 envelope active (¼ oz.) dry yeast
6 tbsp. scalded, tepid skim milk
2 tbsp. apricot jam without added sugar
¼ cup hazelnuts, thinly sliced
Hazelnut-pineapple layer
2 pineapples
¾ cup hazelnuts, toasted, skinned, and finely ground
¼ cup light brown sugar

Sift the flour, salt, sugar, and cinnamon into a bowl. Mix in the orange zest; then, using your fingertips or the back of a wooden spoon, rub in the butter until the mixture resembles fine bread crumbs. Dissolve the yeast in the milk; if using dry yeast, let it stand, following the packager's instructions. Pour the yeast liquid into the flour, and mix to form a soft dough. Knead on a lightly floured surface for two to three minutes to smooth it. Put the dough in a clean bowl. Cover the bowl with plastic wrap and leave it in a warm place for one hour, until the dough has doubled in bulk.

Meanwhile, remove the skin and eyes from the pineapples. Cut the flesh into slices about ¼-inch thick. Remove the core from each slice with a plain cutter. Trim the slices into neat rounds, using a large metal cutter as a guide. Set the rings aside until needed.

Knead the risen dough for one minute, then roll it out into an oblong large enough to fit a baking pan 9 by 13 by ¾ inches. Grease the pan, then place the dough in the pan, pressing it out to fit exactly. Prick the dough well all over. Cover the pan with plastic wrap and leave it in a warm place for 30 to 40 minutes, until the dough has risen slightly. Meanwhile, preheat the oven to 400° F.

Sprinkle the ground hazelnuts evenly over the risen dough. Neatly arrange the pineapple rings, overlapping, in rows on top. Sprinkle the brown sugar evenly over the pineapple. Let the assembly stand for five minutes so that the sugar has time to dissolve, then bake for 30 to 35 minutes, until the pineapple rings have softened and are very lightly browned.

Heat the apricot jam until it boils. Strain it and brush it evenly over the hot pineapple rings. Sprinkle with sliced hazelnuts. Let the cake cool before slicing it.

EDITOR'S NOTE: *To toast and skin hazelnuts, place them in a preheated 350° F. oven for 10 minutes. Wrap them in a towel and rub briskly to loosen the skins.*

Apricot Cake

Serves 16
Working time: about 45 minutes
Total time: about 3 hours

Calories **200**
Protein **7g.**
Cholesterol **25mg.**
Total fat **11g.**
Saturated fat **4g.**
Sodium **75mg.**

1 cup low-fat cottage cheese
¼ cup sugar
1 egg, beaten
1 cup ground almonds
1 lemon, finely grated zest only
16 large apricots
2 tbsp. confectioners' sugar
1 tbsp. apricot jam without added sugar
2 tbsp. pistachio nuts, skinned and very finely sliced

Yeast dough

1½ cups all-purpose flour
2 tbsp. vanilla sugar (Glossary, page 140)
1 lemon, finely grated zest only
4 tbsp. unsalted butter
1 cake (.6 oz.) fresh yeast, or 1 envelope (¼ oz.) active dry yeast
6 tbsp. scalded, tepid skim milk

To make the yeast dough, sift the flour into a bowl, mix in the sugar and lemon zest, then, using your fingertips or the back of a wooden spoon, rub in the butter until the mixture resembles fine bread crumbs. Dissolve the yeast in the tepid milk; if using dry yeast, let it stand, following the manufacturer's instructions. Pour the yeast liquid into the flour and mix to form a soft dough. On a very lightly floured surface, knead the dough for

two to three minutes to smooth it. Put the dough in a clean bowl. Cover the bowl with plastic wrap and leave it in a warm place for about one hour, or until the dough has doubled in bulk.

Knead the risen dough for one minute, then roll it out to form an oblong large enough to fit a baking sheet 9 by 13 by ¾ inches. Grease the sheet. Lower the dough onto the sheet, pressing it out to fit exactly. Prick the dough all over with a fork. Cover the tray with plastic wrap and let it stand in a warm place for 30 to 40 minutes, until the dough has risen slightly.

Meanwhile, heat the oven to 400° F. Put the cottage cheese in a bowl with the sugar, egg, almonds, and lemon zest. With a wooden spoon, beat them together until smooth. Spread the cheese mixture evenly over the risen dough.

Drop the apricots into simmering water for 10 to 15 seconds to loosen their skins. Remove the apricots, then skin, halve, and pit them. Arrange the apricot halves on top of the cheese mixture, spacing them evenly. Sift the confectioners' sugar over the apricots. Let the cake stand for two minutes to allow the sugar to dissolve, then bake the cake for 30 to 35 minutes, until the cheese mixture is set and lightly browned, and the apricots are soft.

Heat the apricot jam in a small pan until it comes to a boil, and brush it over the apricots. Sprinkle them with the pistachio nuts. Allow the cake to cool in the pan. Slice it when it has cooled completely.

EDITOR'S NOTE: *To skin pistachio nuts, drop them into boiling water and simmer them for one minute. Drain the nuts, wrap them in a towel, and rub briskly.*

Coffee Butterfly Cakes

Makes 12 cakes
Working time: about 35 minutes
Total time: about 1 hour and 30 minutes

Per cake:
Calories **180**
Protein **2g.**
Cholesterol **20mg.**
Total fat **9g.**
Saturated fat **5g.**
Sodium **45mg.**

½ cup unsalted butter
¼ cup light brown sugar
3 tbsp. honey
2 tbsp. strong black coffee
2 egg whites, lightly beaten
1⅓ cups all-purpose flour
1½ tsp. baking powder
⅔ cup rum-flavored pastry cream (page 16)
1 tsp. confectioners' sugar

Preheat the oven to 350° F. Grease a 12-cup muffin pan. Dust the cups lightly with flour.

Using a wooden spoon or an electric mixer, combine the butter with the sugar and honey, beating until soft. Add the coffee and 1 tablespoon of warm water, and continue beating until the mixture becomes very light and fluffy. Gradually beat in the egg whites. Sift the flour and baking powder together over the creamed mixture, then fold them in carefully with a large spoon or rubber spatula.

Divide the mixture evenly among the muffin cups. Bake the cakes for 15 to 20 minutes, until they are well risen, springy to the touch, and very slightly shrunk from the sides of the pan. Leave the cakes in the pan for two to three minutes, then transfer them to a wire rack to cool.

Using a small, sharp, pointed knife, carefully cut a cone out of the center of each cake. Cut each of the cones in half.

Put the rum-flavored pastry cream in a pastry bag fitted with a medium-size star tip. Pipe a whirl of cream into the middle of each cake. Replace the two halves of each cone on top of the cream, angling them to look like butterfly wings. Sift the confectioners' sugar lightly over the cakes.

Cherry-Walnut Yeast Cakes

Makes 24 cakes
Working time: about 25 minutes
Total time: about 2 hours and 45 minutes

Per cake:
Calories **140**
Protein **3g.**
Cholesterol **20mg.**
Total fat **6g.**
Saturated fat **3g.**
Sodium **15mg.**

⅓ cup candied cherries, chopped
1 cup dried dates, pitted and chopped
2 tbsp. rum
2 cups all-purpose flour
⅛ tsp. salt
1 cup whole wheat flour
¼ cup light brown sugar
4 tbsp. unsalted butter
1 lemon, finely grated zest only
1 cake (.6 oz.) fresh yeast or 1 envelope (¼ oz.) active dry yeast
1 cup scalded, tepid skim milk
1 egg
4 tbsp. safflower oil
½ cup walnuts, chopped
1 tsp. confectioners' sugar

Put the cherries and dates into a small bowl with the rum and mix well. Cover the fruit and set it aside.

Sift the all-purpose flour and salt into a large bowl. Mix in the whole wheat flour and brown sugar. Using your fingertips or the back of a wooden spoon, rub the butter into the mixture until it resembles fine bread crumbs. Mix in the lemon zest. Dissolve the yeast in the milk; if using dry yeast, let it stand, following the packager's instructions. Whisk the egg and oil together. Pour the yeast and egg liquids into the flour mixture; beat the dough with a wooden spoon or electric beater until smooth and elastic—five minutes. Cover the bowl with plastic wrap and leave the dough in a warm place for one hour, until doubled in size. Grease and lightly dust with flour two 12-cup muffin pans.

Beat the cherry-date mixture and half of the walnuts into the risen dough. Divide the dough evenly into the muffin cups. Cover the pans loosely with plastic wrap and leave them in a warm place until the dough rises to the top of the pans—30 to 40 minutes. Meanwhile, preheat the oven to 400° F.

When the dough has risen, sprinkle the remaining walnuts on top and bake for 20 to 25 minutes, until well risen, golden brown, and slightly shrunk from the sides. Turn the cakes out onto racks. When cool, sift the confectioners' sugar over the cakes.

Banana and Cardamom Cakes

Makes 18 cakes
Working time: about 20 minutes
Total time: about 50 minutes

Per cake:
Calories **145**
Protein **3g.**
Cholesterol **25mg.**
Total fat **9g.**
Saturated fat **2g.**
Sodium **115mg.**

½ cup polyunsaturated margarine
⅓ cup brown sugar
10 cardamom pods, seeds only, finely chopped
1 cup whole wheat flour
2 tsp. baking powder
2 eggs
2 medium bananas, mashed
½ cup ground almonds
Creamy topping
⅓ cup low-fat ricotta cheese
2 tsp. honey
1 tbsp. plain low-fat yogurt

Preheat the oven to 375° F. Grease and flour 18 muffin cups. Cream the margarine and sugar until fluffy, and add the cardamom seeds. Sift the flour with the baking powder, adding the bran left in the sieve. Using a wooden spoon, beat the eggs into the margarine and sugar one at a time, adding 1 tablespoon of the flour mixture with each egg.

Beat in the bananas and almonds, then fold in the remaining flour mixture.

Divide the batter among the muffin cups and bake the cakes for 15 minutes, until the centers spring back when pressed. Loosen the cakes from the pan with a small knife and put them on a wire rack to cool.

To make the topping, blend the cheese with the honey and yogurt. When the mixture is smooth, spoon it into a piping bag fitted with a medium-size star tip and pipe a rosette on each cake.

Cinnamon Rock Cakes

BECAUSE OF THEIR LOW FAT CONTENT, THESE CAKES DO NOT
KEEP WELL AND SHOULD BE EATEN THE DAY THEY ARE BAKED.

Makes 16 rock cakes
Working time: about 20 minutes
Total time: about 1 hour

Per rock cake:
Calories **135**
Protein **3g.**
Cholesterol **25mg.**
Total fat **4g.**
Saturated fat **2g.**
Sodium **90mg.**

1 cup all-purpose flour
2 tsp. baking powder
½ tsp. grated nutmeg
1 tsp. ground cinnamon
1 cup whole wheat flour
¼ cup dark brown sugar
1 lemon, finely grated zest only
4 tbsp. unsalted butter
⅔ cup raisins
⅔ cup golden raisins
1 egg, beaten
2 tbsp. plain low-fat yogurt
6 tbsp. skim milk
2 tsp. sugar

Preheat the oven to 425° F. Grease and lightly flour two baking sheets.

Sift the all-purpose flour, baking powder, nutmeg, and ½ teaspooon of the cinnamon into a bowl. Mix in the whole wheat flour, brown sugar, and lemon zest. Using your fingertips or the back of a wooden spoon, rub the butter into the flour until the mixture resembles fine bread crumbs. Mix in both kinds of raisins, then make a well in the center. Put the egg, yogurt, and milk in the well, and stir to blend thoroughly. The mixture should be fairly soft.

Space heaping teaspoons of the mixture so that they are well apart on the prepared baking sheets. Bake for 15 to 20 minutes, until the cakes are fully risen, golden brown, and firm to the touch. Transfer the cakes from the baking sheets to wire racks to cool.

Mix the sugar with the remaining cinnamon and sprinkle the combination over the cakes.

Raspberry Surprise Cakes

Makes 15 cakes
Working time: about 20 minutes
Total time: about 1 hour

Per cake:
Calories **145**
Protein **2g.**
Cholesterol **15mg.**
Total fat **8g.**
Saturated fat **5g.**
Sodium **35mg.**

½ cup unsalted butter
½ cup light brown sugar
1 lemon, finely chopped zest only
1½ tbsp. honey
2 egg whites, lightly beaten
1 cup all-purpose flour
1 tsp. baking powder
2 tbsp. thickened raspberry puree (page 15)
1½ tbsp. dried shredded coconut

Preheat the oven to 375° F. Grease 15 small, oval, fluted tartlet pans or muffin cups. Dust them lightly with flour.

Using a wooden spoon, mix the butter, sugar, lemon zest, and honey until soft and creamy. Stir in 1 tablespoon of warm water and continue beating until the mixture is very light and fluffy. Gradually beat in the egg whites. Sift the flour and baking powder into the creamed mixture, then fold in carefully with a large spoon or rubber spatula.

Spoon half the mixture into the prepared pans or cups and spread it evenly, then put ½ teaspoon of the fruit puree in the center. Divide the remaining creamed mixture among the pans (or cups) and carefully spread it out to cover the fruit puree. Put the pans (or cups) on a baking sheet. Sprinkle the coconut evenly on top of the filled pans.

Bake the cakes for 15 to 20 minutes, until they are well risen and springy to the touch. Allow them to cool in the pans for two to three minutes, then transfer them to wire racks.

EDITOR'S NOTE: *Other fruit puree or jam without sugar may be substituted for the raspberry puree.*

Spiced Tea Cakes

Makes 12 tea cakes
Working time: about 50 minutes
Total time: about 2 hours and 40 minutes

Per tea cake:
Calories **235**
Protein **6g.**
Cholesterol **30mg.**
Total fat **5g.**
Saturated fat **3g.**
Sodium **30mg.**

2 cups all-purpose flour
½ tsp. salt
½ tsp. grated nutmeg
¼ tsp. ground cloves
½ tsp. ground cinnamon
½ tsp. ground allspice
¼ tsp. ground mace
2 cups whole wheat flour
¼ cup light brown sugar
2 tbsp. unsalted butter
2 cakes (1.2 oz.) fresh yeast, or 2 envelopes (½ oz.) active dry yeast
1 egg, beaten
6 tbsp. sour cream
⅓ cup currants
½ cup golden raisins
2 tbsp. honey

Sift the all-purpose flour, salt, and spices into a large bowl. Mix in the whole wheat flour and brown sugar. Using your fingertips or the back of a wooden spoon, rub the butter into the flour and make a well in the center of the mixture. Dissolve the yeast in ⅔ cup of tepid water; if using dried yeast, let it stand, following the manufacturer's instructions. Pour the yeast liquid into the well and add the egg and sour cream. Mix to form a soft dough.

Knead the dough on a lightly floured surface for about 10 minutes, until it is smooth and elastic. Put the dough in a clean bowl. Cover the bowl with plastic wrap and leave it in a warm place for about one hour, until the dough has doubled in size. Meanwhile, grease and lightly flour three baking sheets.

Punch down the risen dough, then knead in the currants and golden raisins. Divide the dough into 12 equal pieces. Knead and shape each piece into a smooth ball. Flatten them with a rolling pin into rounds (about 4 inches in diameter), and place four on each baking sheet. Prick the rounds well with a fork.

Loosely cover the tea cakes with plastic wrap and leave them in a warm place for about 30 minutes, until doubled in size. Preheat the oven to 425° F.

Bake the risen tea cakes for 15 to 20 minutes, until they are golden brown and sound hollow when lightly tapped on the bottom. Remove the tea cakes from the oven and immediately brush them with honey. Place them on wire racks to cool.

SUGGESTED ACCOMPANIMENT: *thickened fruit puree (page 15) or jam without added sugar.*

Rum Babas

THESE BUTTERY YEAST CAKES ARE TRADITIONALLY SOAKED IN A VERY SWEET SYRUP AND ADORNED WITH CREAM. THIS RECIPE SUBSTITUTES YOGURT FOR CREAM, AND CUTS DOWN ON THE BUTTER IN THE DOUGH AND THE SUGAR IN THE SYRUP.

Makes 12 babas
Working time: about 50 minutes
Total time: about 4 hours

Per baba:
Calories **75**
Protein **4g.**
Cholesterol **30mg.**
Total fat **4g.**
Saturated fat **2g.**
Sodium **90mg.**

1½ cups all-purpose flour
¼ tsp. salt
1 tbsp. sugar
1 cake (.6 oz.) fresh yeast, or 1 envelope (¼ oz.) active dry yeast
5 tbsp. scalded, tepid skim milk
1 egg
2 egg whites
1 orange, finely grated zest only
3 tbsp. unsalted butter, softened
4 tbsp. plain low-fat yogurt, well chilled
3 oranges, zest and pith removed, flesh cut into segments (page 14)

Syrup

1 orange, strained juice only
½ cup light brown sugar
⅓ cup honey
4 tbsp. rum

To make the dough, sift the flour, salt, and sugar into a bowl and make a well in the center. Dissolve the yeast in the milk; if using dry yeast, let it stand, following the manufacturer's instructions. Beat the egg and egg whites together. Pour the yeast liquid and eggs into the well. Cover the bowl with plastic wrap and leave it in a warm place until the yeast begins to bubble—about 30 minutes.

Add the orange zest to the mixture and beat it well for about five minutes, until it forms a smooth and elastic dough. Cover the bowl again and leave the dough in a warm place to rise until doubled in size—about one hour. Meanwhile, grease and lightly flour twelve 3-by-1¼-inch fluted molds.

When the dough has reached the right volume, gradually beat the softened butter into it. Divide the mixture evenly among the prepared molds. Place the molds on a baking sheet and leave them in a warm place for 30 to 40 minutes, until the dough reaches the top of the molds. Preheat the oven to 400° F.

Bake the babas for 15 to 20 minutes, until golden brown, firm to the touch, and slightly shrunk from the sides of the molds. Cool the babas in the molds for five minutes, then transfer them to a wire rack to reach room temperature.

While the babas are cooking, make the syrup. Put the orange juice, brown sugar, and honey into a saucepan with 1¾ cups of water. Heat the mixture gently until the sugar is completely dissolved, stirring occasionally. Boil the syrup for five minutes, until it is thick. Stir in the rum.

Using a small, sharp, pointed knife, carefully cut a cone from the center of each baba. Place the centers on the rack next to the babas. Stand the rack on a large tray. Spoon the warm syrup over the babas and their centers, to drench them thoroughly. Collect the syrup from the tray below and spoon it over the babas repeatedly, until it is all absorbed.

Fill the hole in each baba with the chilled yogurt, decorate each cake with the orange segments, and replace the centers.

EDITOR'S NOTE: *Whiskey may be substituted for the rum.*

Carrot and Raisin Cakes

Makes 18 cakes
Working time: about 15 minutes
Total time: about 1 hour

Per cake:
Calories **135**
Protein **2g.**
Cholesterol **25mg.**
Total fat **8g.**
Saturated fat **2g.**
Sodium **25mg.**

½ lb. carrots, peeled and grated
2 eggs
½ cup honey
½ cup safflower oil
1½ cups whole wheat flour
2 tsp. baking powder
1 tsp. ground cinnamon
½ cup raisins

Preheat the oven to 350° F. Grease and flour 18 muffin cups. Put the carrots in a bowl. Add the eggs, honey, and oil, and mix them together with a fork. Sift the flour, baking powder, and cinnamon into the bowl, adding the bran left in the sieve. Using a wooden spoon, beat the flour mixture and raisins with the other ingredients.

Fill the muffin cups approximately three-quarters full with the mixture, and then bake the muffins for 20 minutes, until the centers spring back when pressed with your fingertip. Loosen the carrot and raisin cakes from the pan with a knife, and transfer them to a wire rack to cool.

Fig Rings and Date Crescents

Makes 24 rings and 16 crescents
Working time: about 50 minutes
Total time: about 4 hours

Per ring:	4 cups all-purpose flour	
Calories **85**	½ tsp. salt	
Protein **2g.**	⅓ cup sugar	
Cholesterol **5mg.**	1 lemon, finely grated zest only	
Total fat **2g.**	½ cup unsalted butter	
Saturated fat **1g.**	2 envelopes (½ oz.) active dry yeast	
Sodium **25mg.**	¾ cup scalded, tepid skim milk	
	1 egg, beaten	
	1 egg white	
	2 tsp. confectioners' sugar	

Fig filling

1 cup (about 6 oz.) dried figs

1 lemon, finely grated zest only

1½ tbsp. fresh lemon juice

1 tbsp. honey

Date filling

¾ cup dried pitted dates

1 orange, zest finely grated, juice strained

½ cup walnuts, chopped

Per crescent:
Calories **125**
Protein **3g.**
Cholesterol **10mg.**
Total fat **5g.**
Saturated fat **2g.**
Sodium **25mg.**

Sift the flour and salt into a large bowl and add all but 1 teaspoon of the sugar. Mix in the lemon zest and, using your fingertips or the back of a wooden spoon, rub in the butter until the mixture resembles fine bread crumbs. Dissolve the yeast in the tepid milk; let it stand, following the manufacturer's instructions. Pour the yeast liquid and the beaten egg into the flour. Mix to form a firm dough. Knead very lightly, on a floured surface, to smooth the dough. Put it in a clean bowl, cover the bowl with plastic wrap, and refrigerate for two to three hours. (The period in the refrigerator makes the soft dough firm enough to handle and allows it to rise very slowly.)

Meanwhile, prepare the fillings. To make the fig filling, put the dried figs, lemon zest, lemon juice, and honey into a food processor and blend them to a smooth paste. Alternatively, chop the figs very finely, and mix them in a bowl with the remaining ingredients to make a paste. Cover the paste and set it aside.

To make the date filling, chop the dates and put them in a saucepan with the orange zest and juice. Heat gently until the dates soften and absorb all of the orange juice. Remove the dates from the heat, mix in the walnuts, and allow the mixture to cool. Cover it and set it aside.

Preheat the oven to 400° F. Grease three large baking sheets. When the refrigeration time is up, remove half of the dough from the refrigerator to make the fig rings. Roll out the dough on a floured surface into a rectangle about 12 by 18 inches. Trim the edges, then cut the rectangle into three equal strips lengthwise; cut each strip crosswise into eight equal pieces. Pipe the fig paste along one edge of each pastry piece, roll up the pastry, and form each roll into a ring *(below)*. Place the rings on baking sheets, with the lengthwise seams underneath. Let the rings stand in a warm place for about 15 minutes to rise.

Lightly mix the egg white with the remaining sugar. Brush half of the glaze evenly over the rings. Bake the rings for about 15 minutes, until they are well risen and golden brown.

To make the date crescents, roll out the remaining pastry to about ¼ inch thick. Cut out oval shapes from the dough and spread a heaping teaspoon of the date mixture down the middle of each oval *(below)*. Roll the ovals up to enclose the filling. Shape the dough into crescents. Place the crescents on baking trays, with the seams underneath. Let the crescents stand in a warm place for about 15 minutes to rise. Then glaze and bake them, following the directions given above for the rings.

Transfer the rings and crescents to wire racks to cool. Sift the confectioners' sugar lightly over them. If possible, serve the rings and crescents warm.

Shaping Rings and Crescents

1 *FILLING THE FIG RINGS. Using a pastry bag fitted with a plain tip about ⅜ inch in diameter, pipe lines of fig paste along one long edge of each rectangle. Roll the dough to enclose the paste, forming a cylinder with the seam underneath. Bring the two ends to join each other, and pinch them together to create a circle.*

2 *ENCLOSING THE DATE STUFFING. Using a 4-inch oval cutter, cut ovals from the rolled dough. Place a heaping teaspoon of date mixture in the center of each oval. Roll each oval lengthwise around its filling, keeping the ends pointed. Shape the dough into crescents and place them seam side down on the baking sheet.*

Fairy Cakes

Makes 12 cakes
Working time: about 30 minutes
Total time: 1 hour and 15 minutes

Per plain, cherry, or golden raisin cake:
Calories **195**
Protein **2g.**
Cholesterol **25mg.**
Total fat **8g.**
Saturated fat **2g.**
Sodium **160mg.**

Per coconut cake:
Calories **205**
Protein **3g.**
Cholesterol **25mg.**
Total fat **12g.**
Saturated fat **5g.**
Sodium **155mg.**

½ cup polyunsaturated margarine
⅓ cup sugar
3 tbsp. honey
1 tsp. pure vanilla extract
2 egg whites, lightly beaten
1½ cups all-purpose flour
1½ tsp. baking powder
1 tbsp. candied cherries, chopped
2 tbsp. dried shredded coconut
¼ cup golden raisins
⅔ cup pastry cream (page 16)
1 hazelnut, thinly sliced
chocolate curls for garnish (page 18)

Preheat the oven to 375° F. Grease a 12-cup muffin pan. Dust the cups lightly with flour.

With a wooden spoon, beat the margarine with the sugar and honey until soft and creamy. Add the vanilla extract and 3 tablespoons of water; continue beating until the mixture becomes very light and fluffy. Grad-ually stir in the egg whites. Sift the flour and baking powder over the creamed mixture, then fold them in carefully with a large spoon or rubber spatula.

Fill three of the muffin cups halfway with the plain mixture. Divide the remaining mixture equally into three parts. To one-third add the cherries, reserving three pieces; to another third add the coconut, re-serving 2 teaspoons; to the remaining third, add the golden raisins. Spoon the mixtures into the muffin cups. Bake for 10 to 15 minutes, until the cakes are well risen, golden brown, and springy to the touch. Leave them in the pan for two to three minutes, then transfer them to wire racks.

When the cakes have cooled, put the pastry cream into a piping bag fitted with a medium-size star tip. Pipe a shell shape on top of each cake. Decorate the plain cakes with the hazelnut slices and the cherry cakes with the reserved cherry pieces. Use the reserved coconut to decorate the coconut cakes. Garnish the golden raisin cakes with the chocolate curls.

Madeleines

THIS RECIPE FOR THE SHELL-SHAPED SPONGE CAKES KNOWN AS MADELEINES USES LESS EGG YOLK AND BUTTER THAN TRADITIONAL MIXTURES.

Makes 20 madeleines
Working time: about 10 minutes
Total time: about 35 minutes

Per madeleine:
Calories **65**
Protein **1g.**
Cholesterol **30mg.**
Total fat **2g.**
Saturated fat **1g.**
Sodium **10mg.**

1 egg
1 egg white
½ cup sugar
1 tbsp. amaretto liqueur
½ cup all-purpose flour
3 tbsp. unsalted butter, melted and cooled
1 tbsp. vanilla sugar (Glossary, page140)

Preheat the oven to 400° F. Grease twenty 3-inch madeleine molds and dust them lightly with flour.

Put the egg and egg white into a bowl together with the sugar and the amaretto. Whisk the mixture until it thickens to the consistency of slightly whipped heavy cream. Sift the flour lightly over the surface of the mixture, and then fold the flour in very carefully with a large spoon or rubber spatula. Gently fold in the melted butter.

Fill each madeleine mold halfway with the mixture. Bake the madeleines for 15 to 20 minutes, until they are fully risen, lightly browned, and springy to the touch. Carefully turn them out of the molds onto a wire rack. Immediately sift vanilla sugar over the madeleines. Serve them at once, while still warm, or allow them to cool.

Raspberry-Filled Shells

Makes 18 shells
Working time: about 40 minutes
Total time: about 1 hour and 40 minutes

Per shell:	3 eggs
Calories **107**	½ cup sugar
Protein **2g.**	¾ cup all-purpose flour
Cholesterol **50mg.**	1 cup whipping cream, whipped
Total fat **6g.**	2½ cups fresh raspberries,
Saturated fat **3g.**	or frozen raspberries, thawed
Sodium **20mg.**	1 tbsp. confectioners' sugar

Preheat the oven to 350° F. Grease 18 rounded 2½-by-1-inch molds and dust them lightly with flour.

To make the cake, put the eggs and sugar in a large bowl. Place the bowl over a saucepan of hot, but not boiling, water on low heat. Whisk until the mixture becomes thick and very pale in color *(page 12)*. Remove the bowl from the heat, and continue whisking until the mixture is cool and will hold a ribbon almost indefinitely. Sift the flour very lightly over the top of the whisked mixture, and fold it in carefully with a large spoon or a rubber spatula.

Divide the cake batter equally among the 18 molds and spread it evenly. Bake the cakes for 25 to 30 minutes, until very well risen, lightly browned, and springy to the touch. Turn the cakes out of the molds onto a wire rack to cool, rounded sides up.

Cut each cake in half, at a slight angle to the horizontal. Cover the bottom halves with cream and raspberries, and set the top halves on the filling at an angle, so that the cakes resemble half-open clams. Sift the confectioners' sugar over the cakes.

Pistachio, Coconut, and Walnut Shapes

Makes 12 shapes
Working time: about 1 hour
Total time: about 2 hours

Per shape:	2 eggs
Calories **130**	1 egg white
Protein **4g.**	½ cup sugar
Cholesterol **45mg.**	¾ cup all-purpose flour
Total fat **9g.**	2 tbsp. unsalted butter, melted and cooled
Saturated fat **3g.**	1¼ cups apricot jam without added sugar
Sodium **20mg.**	⅓ cup pistachio nuts, skinned and finely chopped
	3 tbsp. dried shredded coconut
	⅓ cup walnuts, finely chopped
	2 tsp. confectioners' sugar

Preheat the oven to 350° F. Grease an oblong pan that measures 7 by 11 by 1¼ inches and line the bottom with parchment paper.

Put the eggs, egg white, and sugar in a mixing bowl. Place the bowl over a saucepan of hot, but not boiling, water on low heat. Beat the eggs and sugar together by hand or with an electric mixer, until thick and very pale *(page 12)*. Remove the bowl from the saucepan, and continue beating until the mixture is cool and will hold a ribbon almost indefinitely.

Sift the flour very lightly over the surface of the egg and sugar mixture, then fold it in gently, using a large mixing spoon or a rubber spatula. Gradually fold in the melted butter.

Pour the sponge cake mixture into the prepared pan and spread it evenly. Bake the cake for 20 to 25 minutes, until it is well risen, springy to the touch, and very slightly shrunk from the sides of the pan. Carefully turn the cake out onto a wire rack. Loosen the baking paper, but do not remove it. Place another rack on top of the paper, then invert both racks together, with the cake in between, so that the paper is underneath. Remove the top rack and allow the cake to cool.

Cut the sponge cake in half horizontally. Spread the bottom layer with 2 tablespoons of the apricot jam. Place the other sponge cake layer on top of it, and press the two layers firmly together. Trim the crisp edges from the cake.

Cut a 1¾-inch-wide strip from one of the long sides of the cake; cut four squares from the strip. Using a 2½-inch round cutter and a 2¾-inch star cutter, cut out four rounds and four stars from the remaining sponge cake.

Warm the remaining apricot jam in a pan. Put it through a sieve, then return it to the pan and bring it to a boil. Taking one piece of cake at a time, spear the shapes on a fork and brush them evenly with the hot jam. Brush on only a thin layer of jam: Too much would make the cake soggy. Coat the rounds with pistachios, the stars with coconut, and the squares with walnuts:

Taking each shape in one hand, sprinkle and press nuts or coconut evenly over the surface of the cake with the other hand.

Rest a sheet of paper diagonally across each walnut square, so as to cover half of the square. Sift confectioners' sugar over the exposed sections of the walnut squares, and then sift the sugar over the tops of the pistachio rounds.

EDITOR'S NOTE: *To skin pistachio nuts, parboil them for one minute, drain them, wrap them in a towel, and rub briskly to loosen the skins.*

Pineapple Rondels

Makes 12 rondels
Working time: about 1 hour and 30 minutes
Total time: about 2 hours

Per rondel:
Calories **250**
Protein **5g.**
Cholesterol **70mg.**
Total fat **6g.**
Saturated fat **1g.**
Sodium **35mg.**

3 eggs
1 egg white
⅔ cup vanilla sugar
1 cup all-purpose flour
1 medium pineapple, skin and eyes removed
3 large oranges, peel with pith sliced off (page 14)
⅔ cup granulated sugar
1¼ cups orange-flavored pastry cream (page 16)
¾ cup walnuts, finely chopped

Preheat the oven to 350° F. Grease a baking pan 11 by 15 by ¾ inches and line it with parchment paper.

To make the sponge cake bases for the rondels, put the eggs and egg white in a large bowl with the vanilla sugar. By hand or with an electric mixer, beat the eggs and sugar for five to six minutes above a pan of hot, but not boiling, water, over a low heat, until it becomes thick and very pale *(page 12)*. Remove the bowl from the heat and continue whisking until the mixture is cool and falls from the beater in a ribbon. Sift the flour very lightly over the top of the mixture and carefully fold it in with a mixing spoon or a rubber spatula. Pour the batter into the prepared pan and spread it evenly. Bake for 25 to 30 minutes until the cake is well risen, lightly browned, and springy to the touch. Turn the cake out onto a large wire rack and loosen the paper, but do not remove it. Place another rack on top of the cake, and holding the racks with the cake in between, invert the assembly so that the paper is underneath: If the cake remained directly on the rack, it would stick to the metal. Allow it to cool.

Meanwhile, cut the pineapple into 12 equal slices. Remove the hard center core from each slice with a small plain cutter. Trim the slices into neat rings, using a 3¼-inch round cutter as a guide. Remove the two ends of each orange and slice the remainder crosswise to create four uniform slices. Heat ⅓ cup of the granulated sugar with ⅔ cup of water in a wide, shallow pan. When the sugar dissolves, bring the syrup to a boil and simmer for three minutes. Poach the pineapple and orange slices, in batches, in the sugar syrup for about two minutes—just long enough to soften them slightly. Lift the slices from the syrup with a slotted spoon and transfer them to a wire rack to drain. Boil the remaining syrup to reduce its volume by about half.

Transfer the sponge cake and the paper to a board. Using a 3¼-inch plain round cutter, cut 12 rounds from the sponge cake. Brush each round with the reduced syrup.

Spread each round with the orange-flavored pastry cream, coating the top and sides evenly. Cover only the sides with the chopped walnuts. Lift the rounds off the paper and put them on a large foil-lined baking sheet. Place a slice of pineapple and a slice of orange on each coated round.

To make caramel for a garnish, gently heat the remaining ⅓ cup of sugar in a small saucepan with 3 tablespoons of cold water. Stir the syrup and brush the sides of the saucepan with hot water from time to time. When every granule of sugar has dissolved, bring the syrup to a boil, and cook until it turns to a golden-brown caramel.

Very lightly oil two baking sheets. Allow the caramel to cool slightly, then use a small spoon to trickle it in fine lines across the baking sheets. The caramel will set within seconds. Break it in pieces and pile the filaments on top of each cake.

Strawberry Galettes

Makes 12 galettes
Working time: about 1 hour
Total time: about 2 hours and 10 minutes

Per galette:
Calories **185**
Protein **6g.**
Cholesterol **95mg.**
Total fat **7g.**
Saturated fat **3g.**
Sodium **80mg.**

4 eggs
1 egg white
¾ cup sugar
1¼ cups all-purpose flour
4 tbsp. unsalted butter, melted and cooled
⅔ cup whipping cream
1 tsp. pure vanilla extract
2 tbsp. confectioners' sugar
¾ cup plain low-fat yogurt
1 lb. strawberries, hulled, all but six sliced lengthwise

Preheat the oven to 350° F. Butter an oblong baking pan about 11 by 15 by ¾ inches. Line the base with parchment paper.

Put the eggs and egg white into a large mixing bowl with the sugar. Place the bowl over a saucepan of hot, but not boiling, water on low heat. Beat the eggs and sugar by hand or with an electric mixer until they become thick and very pale *(page 12)*. Remove the bowl from the heat and continue beating until the mixture is cool and it falls from the beater in a ribbon almost indefinitely. Very lightly sift the flour over the surface of the egg mixture, then fold it in carefully with a large spoon or a rubber spatula. Gradually fold in the melted butter.

Pour the sponge cake mixture into the prepared baking pan and spread it out evenly. Bake the cake for 30 to 35 minutes, until it is risen, lightly browned, and springy to the touch. Turn the cake out of the pan onto a cooling rack and loosen, but do not remove, the lining paper. Place another cooling rack on top of the paper; invert both racks, with the cake in the middle, so that the paper is underneath. Remove the top rack and allow the cake to cool.

To make the filling, put the cream, vanilla extract, and 1 tablespoon of the confectioners' sugar into a bowl and beat them until the cream is thick but not buttery. Gently mix in the yogurt. Keep the cream filling refrigerated until you are ready to use it.

Using a 3¼-inch plain round cutter, cut out 12 rounds from the cake. Slice each round in half horizontally. Cut each of the top rounds into six triangles.

Spoon the cream filling into a pastry bag fitted with a small star tip. Pipe three-quarters of the cream filling onto the bottom rounds and cover it with the sliced strawberries. Pipe six evenly spaced rosettes of cream on top of each strawberry-covered round. Halve the reserved strawberries and slice each half into six pieces. Place a triangle of sponge at an angle against each rosette of cream, and slip the reserved strawberry slices between the sponge triangles. Sift the remaining confectioners' sugar lightly over the galettes.

Lemon Marzipan Disks

Makes 12 disks
Working time: about 1 hour and 15 minutes
Total time: about 2 hours and 15 minutes

Per disk:
Calories **300**
Protein **6g.**
Cholesterol **60mg.**
Total fat **15g.**
Saturated fat **3g.**
Sodium **90mg.**

3 eggs, plus 1 egg white
⅔ cup sugar
1 lemon, finely grated zest only
1 cup all-purpose flour
2 tbsp. unsalted butter, melted and cooled
2 tbsp. apricot jam without added sugar, heated and put through a sieve
24 grapes, sugared (page 18)
Marzipan
¾ cup ground almonds
⅔ cup confectioners' sugar, sifted
1 lemon, finely grated zest only
2 tsp. fresh lemon juice
1 egg white, lightly beaten
1 tsp. sugar
Lemon cream
4 tbsp. polyunsaturated margarine
2 tsp. fresh lemon juice
1 egg white
⅓ cup sugar

Preheat the oven to 350° F. Grease an oblong pan about 9 by 13 by 1½ inches. Line the bottom with parchment paper.

Put the eggs, one egg white, sugar, and lemon zest into a mixing bowl. Place the bowl over a saucepan of hot, but not boiling, water on low heat. Beat the eggs and sugar together by hand or with an electric mixer, until the mixture is thick and very pale (page 12). Remove the bowl from the saucepan, and continue beating until the mixture is cool and will hold a ribbon almost indefinitely. Sift the flour very lightly over the surface of the beaten mixture, then fold it in gently using a large spoon or a rubber spatula. Gradually fold in the melted butter.

Pour the sponge cake mixture into the prepared pan and spread it evenly. Bake it for 25 to 30 minutes until well risen, springy to the touch, and very slightly shrunk from the sides of the pan. Carefully turn the sponge cake out onto a cooling rack. Loosen the baking paper but do not remove it. Place another cooling rack on top of the paper, then invert both racks together so that the paper is underneath. Remove the top rack and allow the cake to cool.

To make the marzipan, mix the ground almonds with the confectioners' sugar and lemon zest in a bowl. Add the lemon juice and about one-third of one egg white—enough to make a stiff paste; reserve the rest of the egg white for another recipe. Very lightly knead the marzipan until it is smooth. Wrap the marzipan in plastic wrap and refrigerate it while making the lemon cream.

To prepare the lemon cream, beat the margarine and lemon juice together in a bowl. Put the egg white and sugar in another bowl, and place the bowl over a saucepan of hot, but not boiling, water on low heat. Whisk the egg white and sugar together until they form a stiff, shiny meringue. Very gradually beat the meringue into the margarine in order to make a fluffy lemon cream.

On a surface very lightly sifted with confectioners' sugar, roll out the marzipan into a rectangle a little larger than 7 by 12 inches. Mark the marzipan with a ridged rolling pin, rolling from one short end. Trim the edges, then sprinkle the marzipan evenly with the teaspoon of sugar. Cut across the rectangle to make twelve 1-inch wide strips.

Transfer the cake to a flat surface. Using a 2½-inch plain round cutter, cut out 12 disks from the sponge cake. To assemble the cakes, spread the top of each layer generously with lemon cream. Turn each of the marzipan strips over and lightly brush the smooth side with the apricot jam. Wrap each marzipan strip around a sponge disk with the jam side to the cake. Press the marzipan gently into position and trim it to fit exactly. Decorate the lemon disks with the sugared grapes.

Lemon Curd Cakes

Serves 12
Working time: about 45 minutes
Total time: about 1 hour and 45 minutes

Calories **170**
Protein **2g.**
Cholesterol **60mg.**
Total fat **4g.**
Saturated fat **2g.**
Sodium **25mg.**

3 eggs, plus 1 egg white
⅔ cup sugar
1 cup all-purpose flour
2 tbsp. unsalted butter, melted and cooled
3 tbsp. lemon curd (page 15)
Piped frosting
1¼ cups sugar
1 egg white

Preheat the oven to 350° F. Grease an oblong pan about 7 by 11 by 1½ inches and line the bottom with parchment paper.

Put the eggs, one egg white, and sugar in a large bowl. Place the bowl over a saucepan of hot, but not boiling, water on low heat. Beat the eggs and sugar by hand or with an electric mixer until the mixture is thick and very pale *(page 12)*. Remove the bowl from the heat, and continue beating until the mixture is cool and will hold a ribbon almost indefinitely. Sift the flour very lightly over the top of the beaten mixture, and fold it in carefully with a large spoon or rubber spatula. Gradually fold in the melted butter.

Pour the sponge cake mixture into the prepared pan and spread it evenly. Bake the cake for 25 to 30 minutes, until well risen, firm to the touch, and very slightly shrunk from the sides of the pan. Turn the cake onto a wire rack. Loosen but do not remove the parchment paper. Place another rack on top of the paper, then invert both the racks together with the cake in between so that the paper is underneath. Remove the top rack and let the cake cool. Slice the cold sponge cake in half horizontally, and make a sandwich of the two layers with lemon curd in the middle.

To make the frosting, put the sugar in a saucepan with ⅓ cup of cold water. Heat very gently until every granule of sugar has dissolved, brushing the sides of the pan down with hot water from time to time. Bring the syrup to a boil and cook until its temperature reads 240° F. on a candy thermometer. Meanwhile, beat the egg white until very stiff but not dry. When the sugar syrup reaches the required temperature, immediately beat the syrup into the egg white, pouring it in a steady stream from a height. Continue beating until the frosting just loses its shine and becomes stiff enough to hold a peak.

Without delay, since the frosting begins to harden within a few minutes, spoon the frosting into a pastry bag fitted with a seven-point ⁵⁄₁₆-inch star tip. Pipe the frosting in diagonal lines across the cake. Pipe rows of stars between the lines. Slice the cake into 12 pieces when the frosting has set.

Chestnut and Chocolate Baskets

Makes 12 baskets
Working time: about 1 hour and 10 minutes
Total time: about 3 hours

Per basket:
Calories **230**
Protein **4g.**
Cholesterol **60mg.**
Total fat **8g.**
Saturated fat **4g.**
Sodium **30mg.**

1½ cups chestnut puree
3 eggs, separated
¾ cup sugar
8 oz. semisweet chocolate
1 egg white
3 tbsp. rum
⅔ cup plain low-fat yogurt
1 tsp. confectioners' sugar

Preheat the oven to 350° F. Grease twelve 4-inch tartlet pans and line the bottom of each with a round piece of parchment paper.

Beat the chestnut puree, egg yolks, and ½ cup of sugar in a large bowl until the mixture becomes very pale and thick. Melt 3 oz. of the chocolate in a bowl placed over a saucepan of hot water. Let the chocolate cool but do not allow it to set, then whisk it into the chestnut mixture.

In another bowl, beat the egg whites until they are stiff but not dry. Then, beat in the remaining sugar to make meringue, and gradually fold this into the chestnut mixture.

Divide the chestnut mixture equally among the pans and spread it evenly. Place the pans on baking trays. Bake the chestnut cakes for 15 to 20 minutes, until they are well risen and firm to the touch; a wooden skewer should come out clean when inserted in the center. Allow the cakes to cool in the pans.

Chop 3 oz. of the remaining chocolate. Put it in a small bowl with the rum. Place the bowl over a saucepan of hot, but not boiling, water, and stir until the chocolate melts and is smoothly blended with the rum. Remove the mixture from the heat. When it is cool but not set, fold in the yogurt.

Carefully remove the chestnut cakes from their pans and peel off the parchment paper. (If you used fluted tartlet pans, straighten the sides of the cakes by trimming them with a plain round cutter.) Place the cake rounds at well-spaced intervals on foil-lined baking sheets. Spread the chocolate cream over the tops of the chestnut cakes. Refrigerate the cakes until firm.

To make a paper-thin chocolate wall for each cake, cut 12 strips of parchment paper 1-inch wide and long enough to fit around the cake bases with an overlap of about ½ inch. Melt the remaining chocolate and use a small spatula to spread it thinly over one strip of paper at a time, leaving ½ inch clear at one end for handling. Carefully wrap the paper strip, chocolate side against the cake, around the base of each cake.

Thinly spread whatever chocolate remains on a marble slab or smooth work surface. When the chocolate is no longer sticky to the touch, scrape it off the slab with a knife held at an angle, forming shavings. Sprinkle the shavings over the top of the chocolate cream. Refrigerate the cakes until the chocolate is firmly set—about one hour—then carefully peel away the paper. Sift the confectioners' sugar lightly over the surfaces. Chill the cakes until serving.

EDITOR'S NOTE: *To make 1½ cups of puree from fresh chestnuts, slit 1½ lb. of chestnuts down one side, parboil them for one to two minutes, then shell and peel them. Simmer the chestnuts for about 20 minutes, until tender; drain and put them through a sieve.*

Chocolate Sponge Cakes Coated in Coffee Cream

Makes 10 sponge cakes
Working time: about 1 hour and 15 minutes
Total time: about 2 hours and 15 minutes

Per sponge cake:
Calories **210**
Protein **4g.**
Cholesterol **80mg.**
Total fat **10g.**
Saturated fat **5g.**
Sodium **40mg.**

3 eggs
1 egg white
⅔ cup sugar
¾ cup all-purpose flour
3 tbsp. unsweetened cocoa powder
3 oz. semisweet chocolate, coarsely grated
20 chocolate rose leaves (page 19)
Coffee cream
4 tbsp. unsalted butter
1 egg white
½ cup sugar
1 tbsp. strong black coffee, cooled

Preheat the oven to 350° F. Butter a baking pan about 9 by 13 by 1½ inches and line the bottom with parchment paper.

Put the eggs, egg white, and sugar in a mixing bowl. Place the bowl over a saucepan of hot, but not boiling, water on low heat. Whisk the eggs and sugar by hand or with an electric mixer until thick and very pale *(page 12)*. Remove the bowl from the heat and keep beating until the mixture is cool and a ribbon continues to fall from the beater almost indefinitely. Sift the flour and cocoa very lightly over the surface of the whisked mixture and then fold them in gently, using a large mixing spoon or a rubber spatula.

Pour the sponge cake mixture into the prepared pan and spread it out evenly. Bake the cake for 25 to 30 minutes, until well risen, springy to the touch, and very slightly shrunk from the sides of the pan. Carefully turn the sponge cake out onto a wire rack. Loosen the baking paper but do not remove it. Place a rack on top of the paper, hold both racks with the cake in the middle, and invert them so that the paper is underneath. Remove the top rack and allow the cake to cool.

To make the coffee cream, put the butter into a mixing bowl and beat well until it is light and fluffy. Put the egg white and sugar in another mixing bowl, and place the bowl over a saucepan of hot, but not boiling, water. Using a whisk or an electric mixer, beat the egg white and sugar together until they form a stiff, shiny meringue. Gradually beat the meringue into the butter to make a soft, fluffy cream, then beat in the coffee a little at a time.

Transfer the cake to a flat surface. Using a 3¼-inch oval cutter, cut out 10 ovals from the cake. Spread the top of each with coffee cream. Mark a ridged pattern in the cream with a small spatula, knife, or fork. Spread the sides of each cake with a thin layer of coffee cream, then press the grated chocolate against the sides. Decorate the tops of the cakes with the rose leaves, each secured with a dab of coffee cream.

Mango Slices

Serves 16
Working time:ʻabout 1 hour and 15 minutes
Total time: about 5 hours

Calories **107**
Protein **3g.**
Cholesterol **45mg.**
Total fat **3g.**
Saturated fat **1g.**
Sodium **50mg.**

3 eggs, plus 1 egg white
½ cup sugar
1 cup all-purpose flour
2 tbsp. unsalted butter, melted and cooled
1 tsp. powdered gelatin
1 cup thickened raspberry puree (page 15)
2 tbsp. confectioners' sugar
Mango custard filling
2 large ripe mangoes
4 tsp. powdered gelatin
3 tbsp. cornstarch
1¼ cups skim milk
2 tbsp. sugar
1 tsp. pure vanilla extract
1 egg white

Preheat the oven to 350° F. Grease a 9-by-13-inch pan. Line the bottom with parchment paper.

To make the cake, put the eggs, one egg white, and the sugar in a mixing bowl. Place the bowl over a saucepan of hot, but not boiling, water on a low heat. Beat the eggs and sugar together by hand or with an electric mixer until thick and very pale *(page 12)*. Remove the bowl from the saucepan and continue beating until the mixture is cool and will hold a ribbon almost indefinitely. Sift the flour very lightly over the surface of the mixture, then fold it in gently, using a large spoon or a rubber spatula. Gradually fold in the melted butter.

Pour the mixture into the prepared pan and spread it evenly. Bake for 20 to 25 minutes, until the cake is well risen, springy to the touch, and very slightly shrunk from the sides of the pan. Carefully turn the cake out onto a wire rack. Loosen the parchment paper but do not remove it. Place another rack on top of the paper, then invert both racks together so that the paper is underneath. Remove the top rack and let the sponge cake cool completely.

Line the bottom and short sides of an oblong pan, about 7 by 11 by 1¼ inches, with a double-thickness of foil, allowing it to overlap at the ends of the pan.

Put 2 teaspoons of cold water in a cup, and sprinkle the gelatin evenly over the surface; set the cup aside for a few minutes until the gelatin swells, absorbing all the water. Warm the raspberry puree in a pan, add the gelatin, and stir until it has completely dissolved. Allow the puree to cool a little.

Cut the sponge cake in half horizontally. Set the top layer aside. Place the bottom layer in the prepared pan, trimming it to fit exactly. Spread the raspberry puree evenly over the cake, then refrigerate it while making the mango filling.

To make the mango filling, remove the peel from the mangoes, then cut the flesh away from the pits. Puree the flesh in a food processor or blender; you should have about 2 cups. Put 3 tablespoons of cold water into a small bowl, then sprinkle the gelatin evenly over the surface of the water. Set the gelatin aside while making the custard.

In a bowl, blend the cornstarch with a little of the milk. Pour the remaining milk into a saucepan and bring it to a boil. Stir the boiling milk into the cornstarch, then pour it back into the saucepan. Bring the custard back to a boil, stirring constantly. Reduce the heat and cook gently, still mixing, until every trace of raw cornstarch is gone. Add the sugar, vanilla extract, and gelatin, and continue mixing until the gelatin has dissolved completely. Stir in the mango puree.

Whisk the egg white until it forms soft peaks, and fold it into the mango mixture. Pour the mango custard on top of the raspberry puree and spread it evenly. Place the remaining layer of sponge cake on top of the mango filling, trimming it to fit exactly. Refrigerate the cake for about three hours, until the filling is firmly set.

Loosen the mango custard from the sides of the pan with a small knife. With the aid of the overlapping foil strip, carefully lift the cake from the pan onto a board. If necessary, trim the sides.

Leave two or three long skewers over a gas flame or on an electric burner for five minutes until red hot. Cut the cake in half lengthwise and then crosswise into eight equal sections, making 16 slices. Sift the confectioners' sugar evenly over them. Before separating the slices, caramelize the confectioners' sugar in a lattice pattern with the hot skewers *(page 18)*.

4 *An Austrian kugelhopf fresh from the microwave has cooked to a uniform texture thanks to its traditional ring shape, which allows microwaves to penetrate evenly.*

Cakes from the Microwave

The microwave oven not only bakes cakes quickly, it speeds up the preparation of the ingredients, from precooking fruit to melting fat. The recipes in this chapter, ranging from moist gingerbread squares to airy coconut sponge cakes, demonstrate the versatility of the microwave oven for cake-making.

The results are not quite like those achieved in a conventional oven, since the surface of a microwave cake never browns and crisps; a cake made with light-colored ingredients remains pale. The dark ingredients—molasses, dates, whole wheat flour—in many of these recipes disguise the absence of surface color, but the cakes still lack the crusty top and sides of their conventionally baked equivalents. Microwave dishes are never floured as a preliminary to cooking; this step helps the browning process in a conventional oven, but would leave a damp, gray coating on a microwave cake. In place of flour, graham-cracker crumbs are used to line dishes in several of these recipes.

For making roulades, the absence of brittle edges is a real boon; the hard edges of conventionally baked sponge cakes have to be trimmed before they can be rolled, lest they buckle. The chocolate and apricot roulade on page 138 as well as the raspberry and hazelnut roulade on page 139 demonstrate the professional results that a microwave gives.

One drawback of cakes without a crisp, dry surface is that their appearance can be deceptive. Because the top of a microwave cake still looks wet at the end of the cooking time, the unwary may be inclined to return it to the oven. Resist the temptation: The cake will dry out in seconds.

The recipes have been tested in 650-watt and 700-watt ovens. Although power settings may vary among different ovens, the recipes use "high" to indicate 100 percent power, "medium" for 50 percent power, and "defrost" for 30 percent power. All recipes give instructions for turning the cakes so that they rise evenly; if your microwave oven has a revolving turntable, ignore these directions.

Sultana Kugelhopf

Serves 20
Working time: about 30 minutes
Total time: about 1 hour and 30 minutes

Calories **240**
Protein **6g.**
Cholesterol **70mg.**
Total fat **11g.**
Saturated fat **4g.**
Sodium **180mg.**

1/3 cup graham-cracker crumbs
15 blanched almonds, or 2 tbsp. sliced almonds
1 1/4 cups skim milk
2 cakes (1.2 oz.) fresh yeast, or 2 packages active dry yeast (1/2 oz.)
2 tbsp. sugar
4 cups all-purpose flour
6 tbsp. unsalted butter
6 tbsp. polyunsaturated margarine
3 large eggs, beaten
1/2 tsp. salt
2/3 cup golden raisins
1/2 cup raisins
1/4 cup currants
1 lemon, grated zest only
confectioners' sugar

Grease a 9-inch kugelhopf mold or Bundt pan and sprinkle it evenly with the graham-cracker crumbs. Arrange the almonds on the bottom.

Pour the milk into a bowl and microwave it on high for one minute or until tepid. Stir the fresh yeast into the milk (or reconstitute the dry yeast with the milk according to the manufacturer's instructions), adding 1 teaspoon of the sugar. Put 1 cup of the flour in a bowl and gradually beat in the milk. Cover the batter loosely with plastic wrap and microwave it at defrost for one and a half to two minutes. Let the batter stand until well risen and frothy—about 10 to 15 minutes.

Melt the butter and margarine in a bowl by microwaving on high for about one minute. Add them to the risen batter with the remaining sugar and flour, the eggs, and salt. Beat the mixture well with a wooden spoon. Stir in both kinds of raisins, the currants, and lemon zest; spoon the batter into the pan.

Cover the batter loosely with plastic wrap and microwave it on defrost for eight to nine minutes, or until it has risen to the top of the pan. Allow the mixture to stand for 10 minutes, then microwave it, uncovered, on high for six minutes, giving the dish a quarter turn three times. Let the cake stand for five minutes before turning it out onto a wire rack to cool. Before serving, sprinkle it with confectioners' sugar.

Coconut Snowballs

Makes 12
Working time: about 30 minutes
Total time: about 50 minutes

Per snowball:
Calories **165**
Protein **3g.**
Cholesterol **50mg.**
Total fat **8g.**
Saturated fat **5g.**
Sodium **50mg.**

¼ cup unsalted butter
⅔ cup sugar
4 tbsp. skim milk
2 eggs, beaten
1 cup all-purpose flour
1½ tsp. baking powder
½ cup dried shredded coconut
4 tbsp. raspberry jam without added sugar
2 candied cherries, sliced
angelica, cut into 12 small leaf shapes

Grease the cups of a six-cup microwave muffin tray. In a mixing bowl, cream the butter with the sugar; beat in the milk and eggs. Sift the flour with the baking powder and fold them into the creamed mixture. Divide half of the sponge cake mixture evenly between the cups, and level the surfaces.

Microwave the cakes on high for two minutes, giving the tray a quarter turn three times. When cooked, the cakes will still be slightly moist on the surface. Let them stand for five minutes before turning them out onto a wire rack to cool. Microwave the other half of the sponge cake mixture in the same way.

If necessary, trim the bases of the cakes so that they stand steady. Spread the coconut in a shallow dish.

Put the jam in a bowl with 1 teaspoon of water and microwave it on high for 30 seconds. Put the jam through a sieve, then microwave it on high again for 15 seconds to warm it. Spear each sponge cake in turn with a fork, brush its top and sides with jam, then roll it in the coconut. Top each snowball with a slice of cherry and a green candied fruit "leaf."

Cranberry Muffins

Makes 18
Working time: about 30 minutes
Total time: about 50 minutes

Per muffin:	
Calories **130**	1 cup fresh cranberries, or frozen cranberries, thawed
Protein **2 g.**	1 tbsp. sugar
Cholesterol **20mg.**	1½ cups whole wheat flour
Total fat **5g.**	1½ tsp. baking powder
Saturated fat **1g.**	6 tbsp. skim milk
Sodium **80mg.**	½ cup light brown sugar
	6 tbsp. safflower oil
	1 large egg, beaten
	Golden topping
	4 tbsp. light brown sugar
	½ tsp. ground cinnamon

Put the cranberries and sugar in a bowl. Cover them loosely and microwave them on high for one and a half to two minutes, until the berries are tender but still intact, stirring once. (If cooked for too long, the fruit will collapse when stirred into the cake batter.) Allow the cranberries to cool. Meanwhile, line the cups of a

six-cup microwave muffin tray or six small ramekins with two baking papers each, one inside the other.

In a bowl, sift the flour with the baking powder, adding the bran left in the sieve. Blend in the milk, brown sugar, oil, and egg. Fold in the cranberries, being careful not to crush them.

Using one-third of the mixture, fill the six baking papers halfway. Microwave on high for two and a half to three minutes, giving the tray a half turn after one and a half minutes, or rearranging the ramekins once. Meanwhile, mix the sugar with the cinnamon for the topping. As soon as the muffins have been removed from the oven, sprinkle each one with a little of the topping. Discard the outer baking paper from each muffin and let the muffins cool on a rack. Cook the remaining two batches of muffins in the same way.

EDITOR'S NOTE: These muffins freeze well and can be thawed quickly in the microwave. To reheat two frozen muffins, cook them on high for 30 to 45 seconds, until just warm to the touch. Four muffins need one to one and a half minutes, and six need two to three minutes. Let the muffins stand for three minutes before serving them.

Upside-Down Apple Ring

THIS CAKE, WITH ITS PUDDINGLIKE TEXTURE, IS GOOD SERVED
WARM FOR BREAKFAST.

Serves: 12
Working time: about 20 minutes
Total time: about 35 minutes

Calories **215**
Protein **4g.**
Cholesterol **1mg.**
Fat **10g.**
Saturated fat **2g.**
Sodium **175mg.**

⅓ cup graham-cracker crumbs
2 tart green or Golden Delicious apples, peeled, cored, and sliced into rings
½ cup polyunsaturated margarine
6 tbsp. dark brown sugar
2 egg whites, lightly beaten
⅔ cup low-fat plain yogurt
2 cups whole wheat flour
1 tsp. baking powder
1 tbsp. pumpkin pie spice
1 tart green or Golden Delicious apple, peeled, cored, and grated

Grease a 9-inch flat-bottomed tube pan and sprinkle
it with the crumbs to coat the inner surface. Arrange
the apple slices in the bottom of the pan, overlapping
them slightly. In a large bowl, cream the margarine
with the sugar, egg whites, and yogurt. Sift in the flour
along with the baking powder and pumpkin pie spice,
adding the bran left in the sieve. Fold the dry ingredients and the grated apple into the creamed mixture.
Spoon the batter into the tube pan and spread evenly.

Microwave on medium high for eight to 10 minutes,
giving the pan a quarter turn every two minutes. The
cake is cooked when it feels springy to the touch.
Allow it to stand for five minutes before turning it out.
Serve the apple ring warm or cold.

SUGGESTED ACCOMPANIMENT: *yogurt cheese (Glossary, page
140), sweetened to taste.*

Gingerbread Squares with Crystallized Pineapple

IF THIS GINGERBREAD IS KEPT IN AN AIRTIGHT CONTAINER FOR A DAY OR TWO, THE HONEY IN IT ABSORBS VAPOR FROM THE AIR AND THE CAKE BECOMES DELICIOUSLY MOIST.

Serves 15
Working time: about 15 minutes
Total time: about 1 hour

Per square:
Calories **230**
Protein **4g.**
Cholesterol **35mg.**
Total fat **8g.**
Saturated fat **2g.**
Sodium **115mg.**

2 cups whole wheat flour
1 tbsp. ground ginger
1 tsp. pumpkin pie spice
½ tsp. baking soda
½ cup polyunsaturated margarine
½ cup honey
1 tbsp. molasses
½ cup light brown sugar
⅔ cup skim milk
2 eggs
1 tbsp. crystallized pineapple, chopped

Lightly grease a 7-by-9-inch pan. Line the bottom with wax paper. Sift the flour into a bowl, together with the ginger, pumpkin pie spice, and baking soda. Add the bran left in the sieve.

Put the margarine and all but 1 tablespoon of the honey in another bowl. Add the molasses and sugar, and microwave on high for three minutes, stirring once. Allow the mixture to cool slightly, then blend in the milk and eggs.

Make a well in the center of the dry ingredients and pour in the liquid mixture. Beat well to create a smooth, thick batter. Spoon the batter evenly into the pan and set the pan on an inverted plate in the microwave. Cook on high for seven and a half to eight and a half minutes, giving the dish a quarter turn every two minutes. The gingerbread is done when it is springy to the touch and damp spots have disappeared from its surface. Let it stand for 10 minutes before turning it out to cool onto a wire rack.

Put the remaining honey in a small bowl and microwave it on high for 10 to 15 seconds. To glaze the gingerbread, brush it with the warm honey. Cut the gingerbread into squares and decorate each one with a few pieces of crystallized pineapple.

Date and Banana Tea Bread

Serves 12
Working time: about 20 minutes
Total time: about 1 hour

Calories **145**
Protein **3g.**
Cholesterol **25mg.**
Total fat **6g.**
Saturated fat **3g.**
Sodium **115mg.**

1 cup whole wheat flour
1 tsp. baking soda
2 bananas, mashed
4 tbsp. plain low-fat yogurt
¼ cup light brown sugar
5 tbsp. unsalted butter
1 egg, beaten
2 tbsp. maple syrup
⅔ cup dried dates, pitted and coarsely chopped
confectioners' sugar

Lightly grease a 5-by-9-inch loaf pan and line the bottom with wax paper. Sift the flour with the baking soda, adding the bran left in the sieve.

Mix the mashed bananas together with the yogurt, brown sugar, butter, egg, and syrup, blending well with a wooden spoon. Add the sifted flour mixture and dates, and mix to a smooth batter. Spoon the mixture evenly into the loaf pan. To prevent the ends of the cake from overcooking, wrap a 2-inch-wide strip of foil over each end of the dish. Place the dish on an inverted plate in the microwave and cook on medium for 10 minutes, giving the dish a quarter turn every two and a half minutes.

Increase the power to high and cook for an additional two minutes. Remove the strips of foil, give the pan a quarter turn, and cook for one to three minutes more, until the tea bread shrinks from the sides of the dish. Let the tea bread stand for 10 minutes before turning it out onto a wire rack. Sift a light coating of confectioners' sugar over the cake. It may be served warm or cold.

Spiced Apple Tea Bread

BROWN SUGAR GIVES THIS TEA BREAD THE RICH, DARK COLOR
OF AN OVEN-BAKED CAKE: UNLIKE TRADITIONAL CAKES,
MICROWAVE CAKES NEVER BROWN ON THE SURFACE.

Serves 12
Working time: about 30 minutes
Total time: about 2 hours

Calories **185**
Protein **3g.**
Cholesterol **45mg.**
Total fat **6g.**
Saturated fat **1g.**
Sodium **105mg.**

½ lb. Golden Delicious, Cortland, or Granny Smith apples, peeled, cored, and chopped
4 tsp. fresh lemon juice
⅔ cup all-purpose flour
½ cup whole wheat flour
1¼ tsp. baking soda
2 tsp. ground cinnamon
½ tsp. grated nutmeg
½ cup light brown sugar
¾ cup raisins
4 tbsp. safflower oil
2 eggs, beaten
Apple topping
1 large Cortland or Winesap apple, cored, halved, and thinly sliced
2 tsp. fresh lemon juice
1 tbsp. apricot jam without added sugar

Lightly grease a 5-by-9-inch glass loaf pan and line the bottom with wax paper.

Place the apples and half of the lemon juice in a bowl. Cover the fruit and microwave it on high for four minutes, stirring once. Then, puree the apples in a blender or press them through a fine sieve.

Meanwhile, sift the flours with the baking soda, cinnamon, and nutmeg, adding any bran left in the sieve. Stir in the sugar, raisins, oil, eggs, apple puree, and the remaining lemon juice, and beat the mixture to a smooth batter with a wooden spoon. Spoon the mixture evenly into the loaf pan. To prevent the ends of the cake from overcooking, wrap a 2-inch-wide strip of foil over each end of the pan. Place the pan on an inverted plate in the microwave oven and cook the cake on medium for nine minutes, giving the pan a quarter turn every three minutes.

Increase the power to high and cook for two minutes more. Remove the foil, give the pan a quarter turn, and microwave on high for another one to three minutes. The tea bread is done when it shrinks from the sides of the dish and no uncooked batter can be seen through the bottom of the pan. Allow the tea bread to stand for 10 minutes before turning it out onto a wire rack to cool.

To make the apple topping, toss the apple slices in one teaspoon of the lemon juice in a shallow dish. Microwave the slices on high for one minute, then let them cool. Meanwhile, blend the jam with the remaining lemon juice in a bowl, and microwave the mixture on high for 15 to 30 seconds to warm it. Put the jam mixture through a sieve and then brush half of it over the cake. Arrange the apple slices on the cake, and glaze them with the remaining jam mixture.

Carrot Cake with Walnuts

THE FRUCTOSE IN THIS RECIPE IS ONE AND A HALF TIMES
AS SWEET AS THE SAME AMOUNT OF SUGAR, BUT CONTRIBUTES
THE SAME NUMBER OF CALORIES

Serves 8
Working time: about 30 minutes
Total time: about 2 hours

Calories **230**
Protein **2g.**
Cholesterol **65mg.**
Total fat **12g.**
Saturated fat **2g.**
Sodium **225mg.**

1½ cups grated carrots
⅓ cup safflower oil
2 tbsp. skim milk
2 eggs, beaten
½ cup fructose
¾ cup all-purpose flour
1 tsp. baking powder
1 tsp. baking soda
2 tsp. ground cinnamon
⅔ cup raisins
2 tbsp. walnuts, chopped
confectioners' sugar (optional)

Grease a 7-inch round cake pan or soufflé dish and line it with wax paper.

In a large bowl, mix the carrots well with the oil, skim milk, eggs, and fructose. Sift the flour with the baking powder, baking soda, and cinnamon. Fold the dry mixture into the carrot and egg mixture, and blend in the raisins and nuts. Spoon the batter into the cake pan or soufflé dish.

Put the dish on an inverted saucer in the microwave. Cook the carrot cake on medium for nine minutes, giving the dish a quarter turn every three minutes. Increase the power to high and cook the cake for two to three additional minutes, giving the dish a quarter turn after one and a half minutes. The cake is done when it shrinks from the sides of the dish. Let the cake stand for 10 minutes before turning it out onto a wire rack to cool.

If you wish to decorate the cake, rest a wire rack on top of it and sift a little confectioners' sugar over the cake. Lift off the rack to reveal a stencil pattern.

Grapefruit Cake

Serves 12
Working time: about 30 minutes
Total time: about 3 hours

Calories **240**
Protein **4g.**
Cholesterol **65mg.**
Total fat **8g.**
Saturated fat **2g.**
Sodium **100mg.**

¾ cup golden raisins
¾ cup raisins
¾ cup currants
1 grapefruit, zest finely grated, flesh segmented (page 14) and chopped
6 tbsp. fresh grapefruit juice
6 tbsp. polyunsaturated margarine
½ cup dark brown sugar
2 large eggs, beaten
1½ cups all-purpose flour
1 tbsp. honey

Grease the bottom of an 8-inch round pan and line it with wax paper.

Put both kinds of raisins, the currants, grapefruit zest, and juice in a bowl. Cover the fruit mixture and microwave it on high for three minutes, stirring once. Remove the cover and let the fruit cool slightly.

Meanwhile, cream the margarine with the sugar and eggs until light and fluffy. Fold in the flour and the fruit mixture, blending well. Lastly, fold in the grapefruit flesh. Spoon the mixture into the cake pan and level the surface.

Cover the pan and place it on an inverted plate in the microwave. Cook the grapefruit cake on high for 10 minutes, giving the pan a quarter turn every three minutes. Remove the cover, reduce the power to defrost, and cook the cake for another four to six minutes, or until a skewer inserted into the center of the cake comes out clean.

Let the grapefruit cake stand for 20 minutes before turning it out onto a wire rack to cool. While the cake is still warm, brush the top with honey.

Banana Loaf with Streusel Crumbs

THE FRUCTOSE IN THIS RECIPE IS ONE AND A HALF TIMES AS SWEET AS THE SAME AMOUNT OF SUGAR, BUT CONTRIBUTES THE SAME NUMBER OF CALORIES

Serves 12
Working time: about 20 minutes
Total time: about 2 hours

Calories **245**
Protein **5g.**
Cholesterol **45mg.**
Total fat **11g.**
Saturated fat **2g.**
Sodium **145mg.**

¾ cup whole wheat flour
½ cup all-purpose flour
1 tsp. baking soda
½ cup fructose
½ cup golden raisins
½ cup hazelnuts, chopped
¼ cup safflower oil
1 small apple, peeled, cored, and grated
6 tbsp. skim milk
2 eggs, beaten
2 ripe bananas, mashed

Streusel topping

½ cup whole wheat flour
¼ cup light or dark brown sugar
½ tsp. cinnamon
2 tbsp. polyunsaturated margarine

Lightly grease a 5-by-9-inch glass loaf pan and line the bottom with wax paper. In a bowl, sift the flour with the baking soda, adding the bran left in the sieve. Stir in the fructose, golden raisins, and nuts. Mix the oil with the apple, milk, eggs, and bananas. Add them to the dry ingredients and beat with a wooden spoon.

To make the streusel topping, mix the flour with the sugar and cinnamon. Rub in the margarine with your fingertips or the back of a wooden spoon until the mixture resembles fine bread crumbs.

Spoon the mixture evenly into the loaf pan and sprinkle it with the streusel topping. To prevent the ends of the loaf from overcooking, wrap a 2-inch-wide strip of foil over each end of the dish. Place the dish on an inverted plate in the microwave and cook the loaf on medium for nine minutes, giving the dish a quarter turn every three minutes.

Increase the power to high and cook the loaf for two more minutes. Remove the foil, give the dish a quarter turn, and cook for an additional two to four minutes, until the loaf shrinks from the sides of the pan and no uncooked batter can be seen through the bottom of the pan. Let the cake stand for 10 minutes before turning it out onto a wire rack to cool.

Cheesecake with Strawberries and Kiwi Fruit

Serves 10
Working time: about 40 minutes
Total time: about 4 hours

Calories **175**
Protein **9g.**
Cholesterol **65mg.**
Total fat **7g.**
Saturated fat **1g.**
Sodium **120mg.**

1 cup graham-cracker crumbs
1 cup low-fat ricotta cheese
1½ cups low-fat plain yogurt
2 eggs, whites and yolks separated
1 tbsp. whole wheat flour
3 tbsp. honey
2 tsp. fresh orange juice
½ cup golden raisins, chopped
4 large strawberries, hulled and sliced
2 kiwi fruit, peeled and sliced

Line the bottom of a deep 7-inch round dish with parchment paper and grease the paper. Spread the graham-cracker crumbs on the base and flatten the crumb layer with the back of a spoon.

Put the ricotta in a bowl with the yogurt, egg yolks, flour, honey, and orange juice, and beat with a wooden spoon until the mixture is smooth. Microwave it on medium for seven to eight minutes or until thick, whisking every two minutes.

Stir the golden raisins into the mixture. Whisk the egg whites until they stand in stiff peaks and fold them into the cheesecake mixture. Spoon the mixture evenly over the crumb base.

Microwave the cheesecake on medium for 10 to 12 minutes or until it is just set in the center, giving the dish a quarter turn every three minutes. Let the cheesecake stand until cool, then chill it in the refrigerator for about two hours to make it firm enough to remove from the mold.

Run a knife around the cheesecake to loosen it from the sides of the dish. Put a flat plate over the cheesecake and invert the plate and dish together. Lift off the dish, remove the paper from the cheesecake, and turn it out onto a serving dish. Decorate the cheesecake with the slices of strawberry and kiwi fruit.

Orange and Lemon Ring Cake

THE FRUCTOSE IN THIS RECIPE IS ONE AND A HALF TIMES AS
SWEET AS THE SAME AMOUNT OF SUGAR, BUT CONTRIBUTES
THE SAME NUMBER OF CALORIES.

Serves 10
Working time: about 30 minutes
Total time: about 1 hour and 30 minutes

Calories **225**
Protein **5g.**
Cholesterol **80mg.**
Total fat **11g.**
Saturated fat **2g.**
Sodium **170mg.**

⅓ cup graham-cracker crumbs
⅓ cup fructose
3 eggs, beaten
⅓ cup safflower oil
½ lemon, grated zest only
½ small orange, grated zest only
2 tbsp. fresh lemon juice
2 tbsp. fresh orange juice
1½ cups all-purpose flour
2 tsp. baking powder
Orange garnish and glaze
1 large orange, peel and all pith removed (page 14)
1 tbsp. honey

Lightly grease a 1-quart fluted ring mold and coat it evenly with the graham-cracker crumbs. Put the fructose, eggs, oil, grated zest, and juice into a bowl, sift in the flour and baking powder, and whisk them with an electric beater at low speed for about 30 seconds, until well blended and smooth.

Spoon the mixture into the prepared mold, being careful not to disturb the crumb coating. Microwave the cake on high for four or five minutes, giving the pan a quarter turn every minute, until the cake feels springy to the touch.

Allow the cake to stand for 10 minutes before turning it out onto a wire rack. While the cake cools, prepare the orange garnish. Slice the orange into segments, cutting on either side of the membrane *(page 14)*; hold the orange over a bowl to catch the juice. To soften the segments, put them in a dish and microwave them on high for one to one and a half minutes. Add any juice that escapes from them to the juice already in the bowl.

To make the glaze, combine the honey with the juice from the orange and microwave the mixture on high for 30 seconds. When the cake is cool, brush it with the glaze and decorate it with the orange segments.

Chocolate and Apricot Roulade

ROULADES COOKED IN THE MICROWAVE DO NOT NEED TO BE TRIMMED BEFORE ROLLING BECAUSE THE MICRO-WAVE, UNLIKE A CONVENTIONAL OVEN, DOES NOT MAKE THE EDGES OF THE CAKE CRISP AND BRITTLE DURING COOKING.

Serves 8
Working time: about 50 minutes
Total time: about 2 hours and 15 minutes

Calories **170**	
Protein **4g.**	2 large eggs
Cholesterol **70mg.**	6 tbsp. sugar
Total fat **10g.**	⅓ cup all-purpose flour
Saturated fat **5g.**	4 tsp. cocoa powder
Sodium **100mg.**	½ cup whipping cream
	1 cup plain low-fat yogurt
	¼ lb. fresh apricots, halved, pitted, poached, and skinned (page 14)

Line a 7-by-11-inch shallow pan with lightly oiled wax paper, leaving approximately 2 inches of paper over-lapping at the edges.

Whisk the eggs with 4 tablespoons of the sugar until very thick and tripled in volume. Sift the flour with the cocoa powder twice, then sift the combination over the whisked eggs. Fold the two mixtures together lightly with a spoon and pour the batter into the pre-pared dish, spreading it evenly.

Microwave the sponge cake on high for two and a half to three minutes, until it is just firm in the center,

giving the dish a half turn once. Let the cake stand for three minutes.

Dust a sheet of wax paper with 1 tablespoon of sugar, which will help prevent the moist sponge cake from sticking. Turn the cake out onto the sugared paper. Remove the lining paper. Hold another piece of wax paper under the faucet to dampen it; crumple it up, spread it out again, and lay it on the sponge cake. Roll the cake up from one of the shorter edges, en-closing the paper *(page 31)*. Allow the cake to cool on a wire rack.

Meanwhile, whip the cream until it stands in peaks, then carefully blend in the yogurt. Transfer several tablespoons of this mixture to a piping bag fitted with a medium-size star tip. Set aside a few slivers from one of the apricot halves for decoration. Chop the remain-ing apricots and stir them into the rest of the cream and yogurt mixture.

Unroll the roulade and remove the paper. Spread the sponge cake with the apricot and cream mixture, roll up the cake again to enclose the filling, and place the cake, seam side down, on a serving plate. Sprinkle the roulade with the remaining tablespoon of sugar to cover any surface blemishes. Pipe the remaining cream mixture along the top of the roulade in swirls, and decorate the cake with the reserved apricot slivers. Chill the roulade in the refrigerator for about one hour to make it firm enough to slice. Just before serving, trim the ends of the roll.

Raspberry and Hazelnut Roulade

Serves 8
Working time: about 45 minutes
Total time: about 2 hours and 15 minutes

Calories **180**
Protein **5g.**
Cholesterol **70mg.**
Total fat **12g.**
Saturated fat **6g.**
Sodium **70mg.**

2 large eggs
⅓ cup sugar
½ cup all-purpose flour, sifted twice
⅓ cup ground hazelnuts
½ cup whipping cream
1 egg white
6 oz. fresh raspberries, or frozen raspberries, thawed

Line a 7-by-11-inch shallow pan with lightly oiled wax paper, leaving approximately 2 inches of paper overlapping at the edges.

Whisk the eggs and sugar until very thick and tripled in volume. Sift the flour over the egg mixture and fold it in with a spoon. Pour the batter into the paper-lined dish, spreading it evenly.

Microwave the sponge cake on high for two and a half to three minutes, until it is just firm in the center, giving the dish a half turn once. Let the cake stand for three minutes.

Sprinkle a sheet of wax paper with the hazelnuts. Turn the cake out onto the hazelnuts. Remove the lining paper. Hold another piece of wax paper under running water for a few seconds to dampen it; crumple it up, spread it out again, and lay it on top of the cake. Roll the cake up from one of the shorter edges, enclosing the paper *(page 31)*. Allow the cake to cool on a wire rack.

Meanwhile, whip the cream until it stands in soft peaks. Beat the egg white until it is stiff, and then fold it into the cream.

Unroll the sponge cake and remove the paper; spread the cream over the surface, and dot it with the raspberries. Roll up the cake again and place it on a serving plate, seam side down. Chill the roulade in the refrigerator for at least one hour, until it becomes firm enough to slice. Shortly before serving, trim the ends of the roulade.

Glossary

Allspice: the dried berry of a member of the myrtle family. Used whole or ground, it is called allspice because its flavor resembles a combination of clove, cinnamon, and nutmeg.

Angel food cake: very light cake with a snow-white crumb, it is aerated with beaten egg whites and contains no fat or egg yolks.

Angelica: the stalk of the angelica plant that has been candied in sugar syrup. Cut into delicate shapes, it is used to decorate cakes. Any green candied fruit may be substituted.

Amaretto: an almond-flavored liqueur.

Armagnac: a dry brandy, often more strongly flavored than cognac, from the Armagnac district of southwest France.

Arrowroot: a tasteless, starchy, white powder refined from the root of a tropical plant; it is used to thicken purees and sauces. Unlike flour, it is transparent when cooked.

Baking powder: a leavening agent that releases carbon dioxide during baking, causing cake batter or cookie dough to rise. Ordinary baking powders, as used in these recipes, have a high sodium content, but low-sodium baking powder is available for people on restricted-sodium diets.

Baking soda: a leavening agent in cakemaking, it is activated when combined with an acidic ingredient such as vinegar or molasses.

Barley malt: a by-product of beermaking containing the sugar maltose, which is much less sweet than sucrose. Malt extract has a strong flavor and retains moisture well. It is available in health-food stores.

Buckwheat: Although technically not a true cereal grain, buckwheat is ground into a flour used primarily to make pancakes.

Buckwheat flour: a strongly flavored flour made from roasted buckwheat seeds.

Buttermilk: a tangy, cultured-milk product that, despite its name, contains less than 1 percent milk fat as opposed to the 3.3 percent in whole milk. However, buttermilk often has about twice the sodium of whole milk.

Calorie (kilocalorie): a unit of heat measurement, used to gauge the amount of energy a food supplies when it is broken down for use in the body.

Caramelize: to heat sugar or a naturally sugar-rich food such as fruit, until the sugar turns brown and syrupy.

Cardamom: the bittersweet, aromatic dried seed pods of a plant in the ginger family. When removed from the pod, cardamom seeds may be used whole or ground.

Cholesterol: a waxlike substance that is manufactured in the human liver and is also found in foods of animal origin. Although a certain amount of cholesterol is needed for producing hormones and building cell walls, an excess can accumulate in the arteries, contributing to heart disease. See also Monounsaturated fat; Polyunsaturated fat; Saturated fat.

Cocoa powder: the result of pulverizing roasted cocoa beans, then removing most of the fat, or cocoa butter.

Confectioners' sugar (also called powdered sugar or 10x sugar—its most refined form): finely ground granulated sugar, with a small amount of added cornstarch to ensure a powdery consistency. The sugar's ability to dissolve instantly makes it ideal for cake icings, where a grainy texture is undesirable.

Cornstarch: a starchy white powder made from corn kernels and used to thicken many puddings and sauces. Like arrowroot, it is transparent when cooked and makes a more efficient thickener than flour. When cooked conventionally, a liquid containing cornstarch must be stirred constantly in the early stages to prevent lumps from forming.

Cream of tartar: a natural, mild acid in powder form with a slightly sour taste, used to strengthen beaten egg whites. It should be used sparingly—no more than ⅛ teaspoon to one egg white. Beating egg whites in a copper bowl has a similar strengthening effect.

Crystallized ginger (also called candied ginger): the spicy, rootlike stems of ginger preserved dry with sugar. Crystallized ginger should not be confused with ginger in syrup; the two are not always interchangeable.

Dates: the fruit of the date palm, dates can be bought fresh or dried. When dried dates are specified, choose plump unpitted dates in preference to pressed slab dates.

Dietary fiber: a plant-cell material that is undigested or only partially digested in the human body, but which promotes healthy digestion of other food matter. Also called roughage.

Fat: a basic component of many foods, comprising three types of fatty acid—saturated, mono-unsaturated, and polyunsaturated—in varying proportions. See also Monounsaturated fat; Polyunsaturated fat; Saturated fat.

Fiber: see Dietary fiber.

Filbert: (also called hazelnut): the fruit of a shrublike tree found in Turkey, Italy, and Spain, and in the states of Washington and Oregon. Filberts, which are cultivated, have a stronger flavor than hazelnuts, which grow wild. Both are prized by bakers and candymakers.

Fructose: a sugar found in honey and many fruits, fructose is the sweetest of all natural sugars. It can be bought as a powder and looks much like ordinary sugar.

Gateau: a cake filled with custard, glacéed fruit, or nuts.

Gelatin: a tasteless protein, available in powdered form or in sheets. Dissolved gelatin is used to firm liquid mixtures so that they can be molded.

Ginger: the spicy, buff-colored rhizome, or rootlike stem of the ginger plant, used as a seasoning either in fresh form or dried and powdered. Dried ginger makes a poor substitute for fresh. See also Crystallized ginger.

Glaze: to coat the surface of a tart or cake with a thin, shiny layer of melted jam or caramel.

Grand Marnier: a high-quality liqueur made from cognac and orange peel, which has a distinctive orange flavor.

Hazelnut: see Filbert.

Jam without added sugar: jam that is sweetened by the sugar naturally found in fruit (fructose), rather than by added sugar (sucrose). Once opened it must be stored in the refrigerator, where it will keep for about three weeks. If unavailable, substitute a low-sugar jam.

Kirsch (also called Kirschwasser): a clear cherry brandy distilled from small black cherries grown in Switzerland, Germany, and the Alsace region of France.

Kiwi fruit: an egg-shaped fruit with a fuzzy brown skin, tart, lime-green flesh, and hundreds of tiny, black edible seeds. Peeled and sliced, the kiwi displays a starburst of seeds at its center that lends a decorative note to cake toppings.

Kugelhopf mold: a decoratively fluted tube-cake pan. The tube conducts heat into the center of the batter, ensuring even cooking.

Madeleine tray: a specialized mold with scallop-shaped indentations, designed for making small cakes.

Mango: a fruit grown throughout the tropics, with sweet, succulent, yellow-orange flesh that is extremely rich in vitamin A. Like papaya, it may cause an allergic reaction in some individuals.

Maple syrup: a sweet, golden syrup produced from the sap of the maple tree.

Meringue: an airy concoction made from stiffly beaten egg whites and sugar. It serves as the base for mousses and soufflés; meringue may also be baked in cookie form or as edible containers for desserts.

Mixed candied peel: the peel of citrus fruit, soaked in a concentrated sugar solution. It can be bought whole or already chopped.

Molasses: a thick, dark, strongly flavored syrup, rich in iron and a good source of vitamin B. It is a by-product of sugar-cane refining.

Monounsaturated fat: one of the three types of fatty acids found in fats. Monounsaturated fats are believed not to raise the level of cholesterol in the blood. Some new evidence indicates that oils high in monounsaturated fats—olive oil, for example—may even lower the blood cholesterol level.

Papaya: a tropical fruit, rich in vitamins A and C. Like mango, it may cause an allergic reaction in some individuals.

Parchment paper: a reusable paper treated with silicon to produce a nonstick surface. It is used to line cake pans and baking sheets, and to wrap food for baking.

Passion fruit: a juicy, fragrant, egg-shaped tropical fruit with wrinkled skin, yellow flesh, and many small black seeds. The seeds are edible; the skin is not.

Pine nuts (also called *pignoli*): seeds from the cone of the stone pine, a tree native to the Mediterranean. Toasting brings out their flavor.

Pistachio nuts: prized for their pleasant flavor and green color, pistachio nuts must be shelled and boiled for a few minutes before their skins can be removed.

Poach: to cook a food in barely simmering liquid as a means of preserving moisture and adding flavor.

Polyunsaturated fat: one of the three types of

fatty acids found in fats. It exists in abundance in such vegetable oils as safflower, corn, or soybean. Polyunsaturated fats lower the level of cholesterol in the blood.

Poppy seeds: the spherical black seeds produced by a variety of poppy plant and used as an ingredient or topping in cakes. Poppy seeds are so small that 1 pound of them numbers nearly a million seeds.

Puree: to reduce food to a smooth consistency by mashing it, forcing it through a sieve, or processing it in a food processor or a blender.

Recommended Dietary Allowance (RDA): the average recommended daily amount of an essential nutrient as determined for groups of healthy people of various ages by the National Research Council.

Reduce: to boil down a liquid or sauce in order to concentrate its flavor and thicken its consistency.

Ricotta: a soft, mild, white Italian cheese, made from cow's or sheep's milk. The low-fat ricotta used in this book has a fat content of about 8 percent.

Ring mold or savarin mold: a circular cake pan with a hollow center. Its open center nearly doubles the food surfaces that are exposed to its walls, thus speeding up the cooking time.

Rolled oats: a cereal made from oats that have been ground into meal, then steamed, rolled into flakes, and dried.

Rose water: a flavoring produced by distilling the oil of rose petals.

Roulade: a rectangular sponge cake, spread with filling and rolled up.

Safflower oil: the vegetable oil that contains the highest proportion of polyunsaturated fats.

Saffron: the dried, yellowish red stigmas (or threads) of the flower of *Crocus sativus;* saffron yields a pungent flavor and a brilliant yellow color.

Saturated fat: one of the three types of fatty acids present in fats. Found in abundance in animal products and in coconut and palm oils, saturated fats elevate the level of blood cholesterol. Because high blood-cholesterol levels contribute to heart disease, saturated-fat consumption should be kept to a minimum—preferably less than 10 percent of the calories consumed each day.

Savarin: a yeast-risen cake, soaked in sugar syrup and flavored with rum or brandy. The cake is named after Brillat-Savarin, an 18th-century writer on gastronomical subjects.

Simmer: to heat a liquid or sauce to just below the boiling point, so that the liquid's surface barely trembles.

Skim milk: milk from which almost all the fat has been removed.

Sodium: a nutrient essential to maintaining the proper balance of fluids in the body. In most diets, a major source of the element is table salt, made up of 40 percent sodium. Excess sodium may contribute to high blood pressure, which increases the risk of heart disease. One teaspoon of salt—with about 2,100 milligrams of sodium—contains almost two-thirds of the maximum "safe and adequate" daily intake recommended by the National Research Council.

Springform pan: a round pan with removable sides, designed to hold cakes and desserts that cannot be unmolded.

Streusel: a filling or topping for desserts, usually made by combining flour, butter, sugar, and sometimes spices and nuts to form coarse crumbs.

Tofu: (also called bean curd): a dense, custardlike soybean product with a mild flavor. Tofu is rich in protein, relatively low in calories, and free of cholesterol. It is highly perishable and should be kept refrigerated, submerged in water; if the water is changed daily, the tofu may be stored for up to a week.

Total fat: an individual's daily intake of polyunsaturated, monounsaturated, and saturated fats. Nutritionists recommend that fat constitute no more than 30 percent of a diet. The term as applied in this book refers to the combined fats in a given dish or food.

Vanilla extract, pure: the flavoring extracted by macerating vanilla pods in an alcohol solution. (Artificial vanilla is chemically synthesized from clove oil.)

Vanilla sugar: sugar made by placing a whole vanilla pod in an airtight container of sugar for about a week.

Whipping cream: cream suitable for whipping and having between 30 and 36 percent butterfat.

Whole wheat flour: wheat flour that contains the whole of the wheat grain with nothing added or taken away. It is nutritionally valuable as a source of dietary fiber, and it is higher in B vitamins than white flour.

Yeast: a microorganism that feeds on sugars and starches to produce carbon dioxide and thus leaven a cake. Yeast can be bought either fresh or dried; fresh yeast will keep for up to six weeks in a refrigerator.

Yogurt: a smooth-textured, semisolid cultured milk product made with varying percentages of fat. Yogurt makes an excellent substitute for sour cream in cooking. Yogurt may also be combined with sour cream to produce a sauce or topping that is lower in fat and calories than sour cream alone.

Yogurt cheese: plain yogurt that has been drained of its liquid by placing it in a cheesecloth-lined sieve or in a coffee paper filter, covering it with plastic wrap, and leaving it in the refrigerator for eight hours or overnight. The yogurt cheese should be transferred to a bowl, covered, and stored in the refrigerator, where it will keep for up to two weeks. Two cups of yogurt yield one cup of yogurt cheese.

Zest: the flavorful outermost layer of citrus-fruit rind, cut or grated free of the white pith, which lies beneath it.

Index